AGONY
ATKINS

AGONY ATKINS

Anne Atkins

MONARCH
BOOKS

Oxford, UK and Grand Rapids, Michigan, USA

First published in the UK by Monarch Books
(a publishing imprint of Lion Hudson plc),
Mayfield House, 256 Banbury Road, Oxford OX2 7DH
Tel: +44 (0) 1865 302750 Fax: +44 (0) 1865 302757
Email: monarch@lionhudson.com
www.lionhudson.com

Distributed by:
UK: Marston Book Services Ltd, PO Box 269,
Abingdon, Oxon OX14 4YN.
USA: Kregel Publications, PO Box 2607,
Grand Rapids, Michigan 49501.

ISBN-13: 978-1-85424-725-4 (UK)
ISBN-10: 1-85424-725-5 (UK)
ISBN-13: 978-0-8254-6098-2 (USA)
ISBN-10: 0-8254-6098-0 (USA)

British Library Cataloguing Data
A catalogue record for this book is available
from the British Library.

Printed in Malta.

Dedication

For my father

πᾶς δὲ ὁ ἀγωνιζόμενος πάντα ἐγκρατεύεται, ἐκεῖνοι μὲν οὖν ἵνα φθαρτὸν στέφανον λάβωσιν, ἡμεῖς δὲ ἄφθαρτον.

Paul of Tarsus (1 Corinthians 9:25)

Acknowledgements

I would like to thank a number of people at the Telegraph: Charles Moore for being such a gracious and courteous boss, and Corinna Honan for being so supportive and encouraging; Elinor Mills for her tireless enthusiasm, Lydia Slater for being, along with Elinor, such fun to work with, and George Thwaites for making me laugh so much. I also want to thank quite a few copy takers in the North of England somewhere, resorted to when my computer broke down yet again, for chuckling over my column and agreeing with me as I dictated. And Danielle Bernadelle for being a super friend as well as a great agent. And a heartfelt thank you to all those other wonderful friends who frequently gave me their time and expertise for nothing: Dr Siân Coekin, Rev. Dr. Steve Midgeley, David Kitchin QC, Brigadier Ian Dobbie, Shaun, my father, and many others whose names will come to me in the middle of the night in time for me to thank them in Volume II. Lastly I would like to thank Tony Collins of Lion Hudson, not so much for his endless patience, as for the inspiration and compassion to include a bottle of Lagavulin in a writer's advance.

Contents

Introduction

It was early evening in November. The telephone rang. It was the deputy editor of the *Daily Telegraph*, ringing up to offer me a column. (And, incidentally, solve the financial problems we'd had since the day we got married, as students, over two decades earlier, and Shaun went into the church and I became a writer and we had rather a lot of children.)

About a month earlier, I had been in the press because of a politically marginally incorrect Thought for the Day I had thunk on Radio 4's politically extremely correct Today Programme. Since then, Marge Proops had died, and the *Telegraph* editorial team thought it might be time for a new kind of agony aunt. (Or rather, the original kind of agony aunt the world had when the idea first started, three centuries earlier.) Would I like to give it a crack?

When she had finished speaking, I did something I had never done before. Nor have since, actually. I laughed so much I fell off my chair.

That evening, Shaun and I were having dinner with wonderful, much loved and respected friends, the recently-retired literary agents, Gina and Murray Pollinger: Gina had looked after my first two novels. In other words, I was spending the evening with the three people whose opinions I valued most in the world when it came to my work.

They were unanimous. It was a very funny idea, we all laughed a lot, and all three of them said, 'Don't do it.' For ever afterwards, they said, I would be an agony aunt, not a novelist. It would ruin my writing career, it would be a distraction, it was a lunatic suggestion.

So I did it.

Being an agony aunt is like being a blonde. However much you protest and insist and swear on your grandmother's grave, nobody believes you are genuine. You get your hair colour out of a bottle, and you write letters to yourself. People obviously believe, deep down, that God doesn't make blondes and readers of newspapers don't have problems.

Dr Johnson accused the very first agony column, in *The Athenian Mercury*, of making up its own letters. A few years later its successor, *The British Apollo*, was indicted:

'Hark ye, you Apollo, don't you make questions and answers?' To which the only possible answer was:

'Not at present, really Sir; but should soon take that method if other people's questions were of no more consequence than yours.'

Arguing with readers was also an early feature. In 1704, Daniel Defoe wrote in his magazine, *The Review*, on behalf of his writers, 'They are sorry if they do not please, but are not convinced of the fact … since more of the paper is bought than ever.'

Readers of a certain kind of publication love to complain. One wrote to me, apparently dissatisfied with everything I'd ever written. Or done, in fact:

Dear Anne – I wrote to you supporting the woman who wrote to complain about the state of her vicar's garden, agreeing that he should keep his lawn tidy. Of course, you did not publish it. Sometimes, you show some common sense, but you do not come across as a kind or caring person. I also feel sorry for your poor family. Have they no preferences when it comes to eating? You said before that you give the greengrocer a free hand to deliver what he likes. What about the price? Also, last week, you suggested that invalids should shop by post. Why? How dull. Your other advice to them – that in order to move around unmolested, they should use a bicycle horn – is disgusting. This is advocating positively infantile behaviour.
Mrs B.S., Gloucester

What can one say? I was being paid to give wise counsel:

I don't suppose for a moment you will take my advice, but my column is not compulsory. Why don't you read something else?

By the tenth issue of *The Athenian Mercury*, Dunton, its author, was publicly quarrelling with his correspondents.

'There are some persons who have lately been very angry with us because we have published their letters verbatim.'

This was a problem we experienced too.

An agony column was as new to the *Telegraph* as it was to me, the paper never having had an agony aunt before. As soon as it was launched, the letters came in. The next week, five were chosen and published exactly as they had been written – with the names of the correspondents and all. In retrospect, it is appalling that it didn't occur to any of us that this might not be a good idea; but it obviously didn't strike the correspondents either. Or not until it was too late. One had revealed the intimate details of both his marriages; he had a distinctive name, and I'm sorry to say even the little town he came from was identified. Looking back at his letter now, I am aghast.

He immediately contacted us with his regrets that his name had appeared, and after that both my editor, Elinor Mills, and I determined never to make the same mistake again. But it was sometimes a difficult call to make. Some letters were frivolous, fun, and not personal at all: the writers were clearly happy to be named, just as if they had written to the letters page, and might even feel cheated if their witticisms were published anonymously. Others were confidential, potentially embarrassing, and very personal indeed: we could not land another poor chap in the soup. Happily, many of the correspondents were soon giving us clear instructions as to how they wanted their identities concealed or revealed. And if we were in doubt, we published initials only. But it would seem that we still may have made one or two errors, which I only found out about because of this book – and which, to be honest, still puzzle me.

Copyright belongs to the writer. Obviously, therefore, in order to publish the letters again, I needed to get permission from everyone whose letter I wished to include – or at least make every reasonable attempt to do so. Most fortunately, I had carefully kept, in a box file, every letter I had ever used, so it was a simple (if tedious) matter to write to all the authors requesting permission. The vast majority either didn't reply (the course of action I advised if they were happy for their letters to reappear) or wrote back wishing me well and gladly giving permission. A few kindly updated me on the dilemma they had written about in the first place.

But a handful, not surprisingly, withheld permission. One was a wife whose husband had died since he wrote the letter. One was a lady who couldn't remember what her letter had been about. (There were a number of these, actually. But all the others said that if they hadn't objected at the time they didn't suppose they would mind now.) One no longer had the problem, so no longer needed a solution, thank you kindly.

Another refused on the bizarre grounds that she was disgusted at my making money out of other people's misery. How did she think I lived when she first wrote to me? Should a doctor or dentist not make money out of misery? And how many writers get rich on the advance from a book? (Yes, I know one or two do … I wish I could work out how.) Luckily, her problem wasn't very interesting in the first place.

One in particular I am very sorry not to publish. His dilemma was heartrending, and prompted many letters of sympathy. A reader who ran a charity that dealt with that particular agony gave specialist advice, having professionally diagnosed the problem; another correspondent offered to meet up with him. Before long, he wrote to me (and the readers) again, to say matters were much better as a result. Funnily enough, he and I corresponded again once or twice, privately, over subsequent years. I would have loved to have included his correspondence, as an example of the positive effect an agony column can have: he tells me his life has permanently improved, not as much as he would like but enough for him not to take the drastic action he was considering when he first contacted me. But he thought that, if his letter appeared again (no matter how disguised), there was a renewed and increased risk that others might guess his identity and untold damage be done. Reluctantly, he withheld permission.

But a couple of the respondents intrigued, and considerably disturbed, me.

One said my publishing his identity had caused embarrassment, annoyance, even breakdown of relationships within his family. What made it especially sad was that he had previously been quite a fan of mine. So I looked his letter up, and was utterly mystified. He had written me a one-sentence, amusing and inconsequential letter, joking about the nature of my column: exactly the kind of trivium which indicated that the writer would like to be acknowledged. How could this have had the dire effect on his life that he described? Was there a subsequent, more serious letter? In which case, why couldn't my computer find his name anywhere in my electronic file? Or had he confused the letter that I published in my column with another that he later wrote to someone else's? It didn't seem likely, as he apparently remembered it all so vividly. Or were his wife and children simply irritated at his brief moment of fame? It hardly seemed possible. I remain mystified.

The other letter was even more tantalizing, and devastating. I had wrecked his very existence, the writer said, by mentioning his name. His entire community had seen his letter. It had taken him all the years since to rebuild his life. Writing to me was the worst mistake he had ever made. And he never wanted to hear from me again. He didn't include an address. So far, so … well, not good exactly, but straightforward and comprehensible. Unfortunately, however, his signature at the bottom of the letter was completely and totally indecipherable.

Now, if this is from the man whose name we ran in that very first column, when we made that early dreadful blunder, I can not only understand but thoroughly sympathize. I would have felt the same. No amends can be made for such an error of judgment. All I can do is say sorry, which I do, unreservedly and profusely. But the name, although utterly illegible, doesn't contain any similarity to the name on the letter we published that day. And we never again published someone's name if the topic was sensitive. Nor without permission, if we were at all unsure. Perhaps he deliberately signed his name with a scribble that looks nothing like his name. Alas: I can't write to him for clarification, or to say how sorry I am. So it will have to remain a mystery. If you ever read this, Sir, please accept my most sincere apologies: I hope you will one day find it in your heart to forgive me. But I don't suppose he will ever see these words, because he never wants to have anything to do with me again, and I don't blame him.

Fortunately, almost all of the replies were much happier.

I am rather cynical about my work. It is the healthy effect of living with five children who are far too busy with their own lives, I'm pleased to say, to listen to me spouting on the radio or read my ephemeral jottings in the paper or even glance at my novels that have been inspired by their insights. So when people thank me for my Thoughts for the Day, which they kindly believe must be so influential, a little voice in my head robustly reminds me that no one is going to take the slightest notice of two and three quarter minutes between the burnt toast, the commuter train and the school run on a normal Wednesday at ten to eight.

I assumed the same to be true of my column. Two or three hundred words are not, frankly, going to solve a difficulty severe enough for someone to have sent to me in the first place. So I saw my words primarily as entertainment, in the best sense of the word: to stimulate, challenge, inform and amuse. And pay my children's bills. But probably not to change the life of the original correspondent. He or she would eventually have to find a doctor, or shrink, or marriage counsellor to tackle the problem properly.

I couldn't have been more wrong. And again, this only came to light as a result of my asking correspondents for their copyright. A few had kindly given me feedback at the time, to be fair. My advice had been taken, the difficulty solved, the customer highly satisfied. I had supposed this to be the very rare exception. But I had underestimated the power of seeing one's own problem in print, in a fairly prominent part of a prominent paper. It really did change the lives of quite a number who wrote to me. (And I mean change them for the better – not just the unfortunate in the first week whose name should never have appeared.)

I have a letter in front of me as I write. Its author was having difficulty with an intransigent wife and disobedient daughters. Apparently I told him to negotiate – but he gave me credit for the cartoon that accompanied my words, of a man on the warpath with a rolling pin. This was nothing to do with me, but it seems to have done the trick. He stuck it on the fridge and the women in his life miraculously stepped into line. He calls his charmed existence since then, PA (Post Anne).

So, was I right to reject the advice given me over that intimate supper, and start dishing advice out to others?

Well, there were certainly happy outcomes as a result of my decision. Many people loved the column, and often told me so. I was reliably informed that the Revd Dick Lucas, the preacher I most admire in the world (after Shaun, of course) used to recommend to his (substantial) congregation in St Helen's, Bishopsgate, that they should all buy the *Telegraph* on a Friday.

Once, when we were on holiday as a family, on the Kennet and Avon Canal, I stuck my head out of the narrow boat window into a gloriously sunny dawn. Another vessel was just coming to life. Its occupant and I greeted each other. Actually, I think we only just avoided colliding.

'You're Agony Atkins, aren't you?' he said cheerfully.

'Yes,' I said.

'Good stuff.' It was a very jolly moment, and felt like something out of the Jerome K. Jerome that Shaun was reading to us every night.

My father enjoyed the column greatly, which was a good enough reason to write it, and my parents switched their allegiance to the *Telegraph*. As a classicist, he particularly enjoyed the appropriateness of the name I was given, Agony, from ἀγών, struggle or fight; aptly describing one who contends with the world, as a Christian should. (The 'pain' we associate with the word comes from the internal battles we sometimes have within ourselves, as Jesus had when he suffered his ἀγώνια in the Garden of Gethsemane.)

Ἀγών also means a trial for the prize, which is how St Paul depicts the Christian life; or entering into danger for the sake of victory. And because it suggests a gathering – as the people would assemble to watch the competitive challenge – it also implies dispute, discussion and debate.

But the overall meaning is one of contest.

'Yes, it fits you well,' my father concluded.

But Gina and Murray were right about one thing. After my contractual obligations for my third novel were fulfilled, my pen fell silent. I put this down to family pressure:

one of our children was diagnosed with Special Educational Needs; another became acutely ill for several years. But the other day, as Shaun and I were discussing why I haven't written a novel since and how I can remedy the situation, he said, as husbands do, 'Well, you wouldn't listen. Murray and Gina told you what would happen.'

Perhaps the three of them were right.

So now it is my own particular dilemma that I must address myself to solving ...

Anne Atkins, Oxford, 2005

1. If It's Wrong, Stop Doing It

Every agony aunt's page has to contain agonized questions about sex. Mine was no exception.

First, though, I should perhaps explain a bit of background.

There was something of a fuss when the column first started. Cassandra Jardine, from the *Telegraph*, came over to our hectic Victorian vicarage for the day to interview me, in order to introduce me to the readers. As it happens, it was one of those classic days that you can only quite believe if you've lived in a vicarage yourself. (Or an English prep school headmaster's house. Or presumably an embassy in a minor, rather badly run Eastern European republic. Or Clapham Junction.) Shaun had a dozen members of his preaching group over for the day; the children all seemed to have music lessons going on simultaneously; the doorbell and telephone never stopped ringing; a number of unemployed youths tried to sell us co-ordinating dusters in convoy; and as far as I remember, Cassandra and I ended up sharing our soup with several tramps who were all regulars.

That evening a neighbour, who was both a close friend and the deputy editor of a significant newspaper, happened to call too. When I described the chaos that Cassandra had tried to record me through, she said the interview would doubtless be an hilarious account of life at the Clergy Home for the Mentally Bewildered, since living in a vicarage was such an obvious training for writing an agony column. Most disappointingly, however, Cassandra's article, a few days later, read as though we'd had a perfectly normal conversation in the cool of an hotel lobby.

As soon as it appeared, though, other journalists tried to get hold of me. One was Polly Toynbee. Polly's name had all the gravitas, for me, of a childhood heroine – I used to love her jottings in the *Radio Times* – but though she must have tried to contact me a dozen times, my agent told me on no account whatsoever was I to speak to her. (I'm convinced she only stopped ringing because my agent eventually told her that I'd gone to Swaziland on a weekend's Girl Guides' training, and I was out of range.) 'She's doing a hatchet job on you,' she said. 'As long as you don't talk to her, she'll have absolutely nothing to go on.'

So it proved. I found the resulting piece delightfully funny – particularly the cartoon of me, which depicted an ancient harridan in a witch's hat. And she'd clearly had to take her material entirely from Cassandra's article, so all her objections to me were rather lame. A few weeks later I was on a radio programme with Polly: the first time I ever met her. She glanced briefly at me; we were introduced; she turned and stared, eyes widening. I thanked her for her article, and said, quite truthfully, that I had much enjoyed it.

I swear she almost blushed.

For a moment she could even have been lost for words. Then she said, somewhat falteringly, 'I'm afraid the artist didn't really know what you looked like ... '

She was not the only one to object to my appointment. That summer I was speaking at Greenbelt, the Christian music festival, and found myself addressing the most antagonistic crowd I've ever experienced: several hundred, a significant number of whom had obviously prearranged to walk out noisily at regular intervals, while others quizzed me belligerently as to what my qualifications were for the job.

But I suspect the protests had started much earlier. In the first few weeks, a number of the questions seemed almost like clichéd moral dilemmas, as if from a school ethics paper.

This one, for instance:

DEAR ANNE – I am fifteen and have been going out with my boyfriend for ten months. Last week, we slept together for the first time, I am ashamed to say we did not use any contraception; it was late, we'd been drinking. I don't regret the sex. We're pretty mature for our ages and serious about each other. But as it is bound to happen again, I think I should go on the Pill. My mother would die if she knew, so I can't go to our family doctor. Will a clinic give me a prescription without my parents' approval?

Name and address supplied

The simple answer is yes. You can go to your GP, or a clinic, in confidence. At either, a doctor is obliged to try to persuade you to involve your parents, and to consider whether the Pill is appropriate. In practice, you won't have any trouble getting hold of it and telling whoever gives it to you that you don't want your family to know.

But if you are really mature for your age, it's time you answered some hard questions. Why would your mother 'die' if she knew? Do you really think it's because she doesn't love you or care about your welfare? Why do you suppose it's against the law for you to have sex at your age? Is it just because some old fogies who've never done it are trying to spoil it for everyone else? And if you go on the Pill, what's to protect you from sexually transmitted diseases? Or from any other, more emotionally complicated, consequences of your relationship? Are you aware that the majority of girls who have underage sex (who all, incidentally, believe they are mature for their age) later wish they hadn't – and those are just the ones who admit to regretting it.

You will do what you want, and if you're going to have sex it's obviously better that you don't get pregnant. But first you should seriously consider whether you wouldn't be better off with your mother's help rather than mine. I expect she'd live through the shock.

I felt privileged to have the opportunity, not only to advise the individual, but also to put forward what I hoped was a Christian world view. But some of the questions seemed almost too obvious, like whatever it's called in cricket when bowlers send a straight ball directly towards the bat. They were also rather similar to one another:

DEAR ANNE – Recently, I met a woman and was completely overwhelmed by my feelings of attraction towards her. Since then, we have met in secret at every available moment. What I am doing is very wrong, I know, but I cannot suppress my feelings and I want to spend the rest of my life with her. I have never felt this way before towards another woman and neither has she. My husband doesn't suspect anything as we have been happily married for more than eight years. Although I am a devout Christian, everything I believe in has been turned upside down. God teaches us that the most important thing in life is love and now I know what love is. I feel very alone and there is no one I can turn to for advice. Please help.
H.G. (Mrs), Enfield

You now know what *erotic* love is, which is not the same thing at all. God's love means faithfulness, integrity, truth and ultimately self-sacrifice, not the tidal wave of feelings you are experiencing. Naturally, you can't suppress these, but you can resist them. You have written to me for advice, but you don't need it: if you believe what you are doing 'is very wrong', then *stop doing it*. It is the most obvious thing in the world. You'll go on having the feelings (for a while) but you don't need to continue acting on them.

The sex of the person you've fallen in love with is irrelevant. If you have a Christian commitment to your marriage, and you find yourself attracted to someone else, give yourself a chance: stop seeing the other person immediately. Obviously, this is bound to hurt, so be kind to yourself, and get support if possible. If you have a good, sympathetic vicar, no doubt he'll help you through; and anything said to him would be in complete confidence.

And on a similar theme:

DEAR ANNE – My girlfriend and I have been living together for four years, and she is desperate for us to have a baby. However, I am not yet ready to settle down as I still feel young and have a life to lead. I don't want to lose her, but I am worried that she will leave me if I say no. What shall I do? I would particularly appreciate your advice as I am also a Christian and believe in the importance of the family.
Female name and address supplied

You are trying to juggle things which are incompatible with each other. You want a relationship with someone who wants a baby, but you also want your carefree existence. Rather more crucially, you want a relationship with God, but you also want a relationship God has condemned. As you say you are a Christian, you need to do some radical, and Biblical, rethinking to discover what kind of 'family' is compatible with your faith. The heart of the God-created family is one man and one woman who commit themselves to one another for life (Genesis 2). There are some deviations which are tolerated in scripture but which are not ideal – for instance, polygamy and divorce – and some that are not tolerated at all, including adultery and homosexuality (Romans 1:27). The Bible says that you cannot have both intimacy with God and sexual intimacy with someone of your own sex.

The decision to put Christ first is never easy, but always worth it: there can be few people in the world more miserable than a half-hearted Christian.

DEAR ANNE – This 'couple' of women living together are obviously intending to bring a child into a world in which he or she will not know his father or paternal grandparent. There is enough heartbreak already when married couples split up and children are separated from grandparents as well as one parent. It can't be right to make artificial insemination available to couples like this. The welfare of the child should be put first.
Michael Feaver,
Tunbridge Wells

And still in the same vein:

DEAR ANNE – I am 54 years old and separated from my wife of 17 years, although as she is a Roman Catholic, she wants us to remain married. One of the reasons our marriage broke down was my (secret) knowledge that I am homosexual. In 1969, I

acted on these instincts for the first and only time and I still feel guilty. However, recently I have met a 41-year-old man, whom I love very much. He feels the same way and would like to move in with me. To date, our relationship has been platonic, but he would like it to go further and I would, too, I think. Should I begin a 'full' relationship with him – in the hope that I can live out my life as part of a loving couple? Or should I continue to lead a celibate life and risk a lonely old age? Your Christian perspective would help.

Because of the lesson Elinor and I had learned, a week or two earlier, when the name of one of the first correspondents was published and he subsequently wished it hadn't been, we were now being much more careful. As this reader had given us his full name and address it shouldn't have proved difficult to trace him, so Elinor said she would check that he didn't mind all these details appearing in print. She contacted the block of flats where he lived, but he wasn't there so we concluded he must have gone away for Christmas. Well, we surmised that you would hardly write to the agony aunt of a newspaper without expecting your letter to appear, so we decided to go ahead, though naturally withholding his name. We ended his letter with the words 'Name and address supplied', which were becoming familiar.

You specifically ask for a Christian perspective, so that is what I shall give you. According to the law and the Church, you are still married. When you made your original vows, you promised to stay faithful to your wife. An important aspect of Christianity is the recognition that we all fail. But we shouldn't aim to fail, and the ideal is marital fidelity. Nevertheless, deep and loving friendships between people of the same sex – for instance, that between David and Jonathan in the Old Testament – can be a great source of support and joy.

But there is nothing in the Bible to suggest that the 'full' relationship you envisage with this man is acceptable to God, and plenty to tell us it isn't (for example, 1 Corinthians 6:9–10 or Romans 1:27). That's the bad news. The good news is that, in my experience, and the experience of many Christians I know, following God's precepts – particularly when they seem harsh at the time – often results in untold and unexpected blessings. God is good and wise and knows better than we do how we should live. Support is available from Christian organisations which provide counselling for homosexuals, such as The True Freedom Trust 0151 653 0773 (www.truefreedomtrust.co.uk) and Encourage (www.encouragetrust. org.uk). If I were inclined to bet, I should put money on your having a more happy and companionable old age if you hold fast to God's laws. Ultimately, though, the Christian perspective is that your old age is not the end. There is a far better life to come than we can even imagine. It must be worth the wait.

It was after the letter appeared that we discovered the truth. Elinor must have tried again, or left a contact number with the curator of the flats, or something. Anyway, the week after Christmas we learnt that no one of that name existed at that address.

It was then that I realised that people were actually going to the trouble of orchestrating fake letters in protest at my Christian stance – though only on sexual matters; and to what end, I still cannot work out, since they were simply giving me more scope for reiterating the very views that they found offensive.

When I realised that this correspondent was imaginary, I felt strangely bereft. I had agonized over his lonely dilemma, and had even been praying for him … and he was nothing but a fictional creation.

There were, however, other – genuine, and therefore rather more interesting – dilemmas on the same subject:

DEAR ANNE – Friends of ours have just been told by their dearly loved 28-year-old son that he is homosexual. They live in a closely knit rural part of Ireland, where they are pillars of the church and the community, and their son's news has come as a shock. How, as Christians, can we best help them to cope with this?
Name and address supplied

Arguably the most important thing parents ever do for their children is accept them, unconditionally, regardless of any external circumstances or internal developments. After all, this is what God does for us. This means loving our children because of who they are, not in spite of it. Your friends' son now defines himself, at least in part, by his sexual orientation. The most constructive thing you can do is to appreciate him for who he is, and encourage his parents to do likewise. A friend of mine, involved in Christian homosexual counselling (himself both homosexual and a Christian, and therefore celibate) has told me that the reason it is so liberating to 'come out of the closet' is because heal-ing starts with self-acceptance, and self-acceptance with honesty. This young man has just been extremely honest with his parents, and in doing so has made himself exceptionally vulnerable. It is of crucial importance that they take this opportunity to affirm him and tell him how much they love him. As their friends, you should do the same.

Obviously this doesn't necessarily mean you approve of giving sexual expression to homosexual love. Christians cannot condone any sex outside marriage, of any kind. But this is probably not the time to say so. If your friends' son is not a Christian, your attitude towards him should not differ from your attitude towards anyone else with a different moral code. No doubt, you have other unmarried, sexually active friends whom you love – even if you don't agree with their way of life.

However, there is one very important difference. Your friends' son will almost certainly experience far more prejudice than heterosexuals ever do. He will need your support and uncritical acceptance all the more.

However, we had become wary of any problem that seemed too far-fetched. We were both convinced that the following was a set-up.

Nevertheless we rang the person of the correct name at the address given, and spoke to a woman who was clearly in her eighties if she was a day, and absolutely genuine:

DEAR ANNE – I am an 81-year-old woman who has been twice widowed; recently, I became very friendly with my next-door neighbour, who is 72. We were very attracted to each other from the start, but when he started talking about marriage, I refused him, chiefly because my health is not good and I could not cope with being a housewife again. (Too much like hard work!) Since then, he has become very friendly with several other women, but whenever we meet, he is still very amorous and constantly asks me to have sex. I admit to feeling tempted, but do not really approve of extra-marital sex. Am I being too old-fashioned? G.S. (Mrs), Haslemere

Yes, I think in one respect you are. I see no reason, nowadays, why you should have to become a housewife again. Your friend is younger than you, and presumably fitter. He has looked after himself perfectly well until now, so why on earth should you do his domestic chores for him? Why not marry him on the condition that he looks after you? If he agrees, you should have a highly enjoyable future ahead: it sounds as if you'll have a great time in bed, at any rate, and at your age, you can justify spending plenty of time there.

"When you've finished that there's the shopping, cooking, cleaning and ironing. If you have any energy after that we'll talk again!"

But, oh dear, this – like many more to come, I'm sure – was clearly the Wrong Answer.

DEAR ANNE – I was very disappointed with your reply to my letter in February, when you suggested I marry my friend. At 72, he may be nine years younger than me, but he has even more serious health problems than I do and, as he is now grumbling about doing his own cleaning, shopping, cooking, washing and ironing, he certainly would not want to look after me! I have been on my own for more than nine years, really enjoy my life and do not want to change it. I wanted your opinion, as one Christian to another, on extra-marital sex between two elderly, free people. G.S., Haslemere

Now I know more about your friend (and yourself), I agree that the invitation to become his laundry maid deserved the response that you gave it.

My understanding of the Bible is that God created sex for one specific, unique relationship: that between a man and a woman who give themselves to each other for life. In the account of Adam and Eve, the two are one, forged from the same body: 'Bone of my bone,' Adam says, 'and flesh of my flesh.' In God's created design, sex and marriage are inseparable. When this is put into practice, it works for society and for individuals: why go against the Maker's instructions? If you don't want the cake, don't eat the icing. He's a good friend, and I suggest you keep it that way.

Naturally I offended readers (or Polly Toynbee, anyway) by being too restrictive on the subject of extra-marital sex. But I also somehow managed to offend readers by not being restrictive enough:

DEAR ANNE – I think my boyfriend is seeing someone else.
Helen, London NW1

Then see a few more boyfriends.

DEAR ANNE – As a twenty-year-old Christian student, I felt it was inappropriate of you to tell Helen, who thinks her boyfriend is seeing someone else, to 'see a few more boyfriends'. Infidelity needs no encouragement from Christian columnists (although I do think your column is usually great).
Anonymous

Dear me: what did you think I was suggesting? Has the word 'see' now become another euphemism – such as 'sleeping with', which means anything but? When I said see, that was exactly what I meant.

As a Christian, you should know that sex, like fidelity, is for marriage. If 'see' meant what you clearly thought it did, she shouldn't have been 'seeing' her boyfriend in the first place.

Naturally, sexual questions are not necessarily confined to the sexually active.

DEAR ANNE – My daughter is eight, and has always been mature and sensible for her age. So far, she has shown little interest in the 'facts of life', and I have not told her about them as I want her to remain innocent for as long as possible. However, my friends' children of a comparable age are fully informed about every-thing relating to sex, pregnancy and periods, and I am worried they will pass that information on to my daughter. I am begin-ning to feel in the minority on this, and would appreciate your views on the subject.
A.L., Lincolnshire

Sadly, modern parents receive so much criticism that we often find it hard to trust our instincts; on an issue like this, what feels appropriate to you is probably best for your child.

I told our eldest the 'facts of life' when she was about two as I believe that when sex is enjoyed in the context of a committed, life-long relationship, it is not only great fun but thoroughly good, healthy and natural. So I saw nothing in this knowledge that would threaten my child's wellbeing, sense of security, or innocence. I was in a minority, as you are: fellow parents criticized my approach, saying that the 'experts' warn we shouldn't tell children things before they ask us. But I reasoned that my daughter hadn't asked me whether traffic was dangerous, or whether there was a God, or whether I loved her, but I had answered all those questions. You should have confidence in what comes naturally to you.

However, to some extent your friends have forced your hand, and it is much better for your daughter to learn about sex accurately from you, in your chosen moral context, than inaccurately from her friends in whatever context they have picked up their information.

And don't confuse innocence with ignorance. One of my most treasured images of childhood was our five-year-old lying in front of the fire reading a book about sex to her brothers, aged four and two, and explaining it to them. The three of them had no shame, or embarrassment, or prurience, but a truly innocent interest and delight in the way God, and parents, make babies.

DEAR ANNE – I was astonished to learn that you allowed your pre-school children to read a book about sex. What on earth was it?
H.H., Hertfordshire

Yes; it's a disgrace, and sadly isn't going to be reprinted.

Who Made Me? Written by Malcolm and Meryl Dooney, illustrated by Butterworth and Inkpen, written especially for little children, and wonderful.

DEAR ANNE – Apparently, *Who Made Me?*, the book you recommended for children, has been out of print for some time.
Mrs J. Rasmussen, York

"Well, you get a bird and a bee..."

Then there is sex that goes wrong, even within a committed relationship:

DEAR ANNE – We have always answered our children's questions about sex honestly, so when my 12-year-old daughter asked me whether I found sex enjoyable, I replied that although I had never enjoyed it myself, some women and most men did. I explained that the act of making love was not just to create children – it is an essential, symbolic part of marriage, done out of love for the other person.

When my husband heard of our conversation, he exploded with rage. He said that it was bad enough my having these attitudes, without his daughter going the same way. He added that I am boring in bed and said he is only faithful to me because we are married. I have never deprived him, even when pregnant and breastfeeding. Where have I gone wrong?
Name and address supplied

By hurting him in the most personal, painful way you possibly could. I, too, believe in total honesty with children. But there are a few things that they do not need or want to know. If you and your husband have problems with your sex life – and I believe you do – it is disloyal to tell anyone other than a professional, who can help you solve them. How do you suppose your husband feels, knowing that you have to grit your teeth to endure his lovemaking? And now that his own daughter knows, too, his humiliation is complete.

Everything you have said about sex is true. It is precisely because it is a symbolic act that it is so important – illustrating, among other things, the exclusive love you have for each other. This also means that you should sometimes shut the bedroom door and keep the children out of your secrets.

If you truly love your husband, I suggest you apologize. Then go straight to your GP and ask to be referred to a sex counsellor.

DEAR ANNE – After an unhappy marriage, I played the field for some years, enjoying a veritable string of one-night stands. Quite unexpectedly, one of these turned into a genuine long-term affair. After two and a half years, we are still very much in love.

Because of this, we quickly established openness and trust, so a few months ago I told her about my previous affairs. She said how wonderful it was that she could now be totally frank with me, and then told me all, too. She left me speechless. There is hardly anyone I know with whom she has *not* had sex.

I tried not to show my shock. Her revelations haven't affected my love for her, and I know that it is unreasonable to have double standards, but the experience has rendered me completely impotent. I can't get over it. My illogical Stone Age reaction is driving me nuts. We have talked and talked about it, and I have been to my GP, but I know that this is not a physical problem. I don't want therapy because the idea makes me feel like a weirdo. Any thoughts?
Name and address supplied

You have to decide whether you're a New Man or a Cave Man. You can't be both. New Man has plenty of time for herbal teas and counselling. 'I have a problem you can help me with,' he tells his shrink, then obediently lies down on the couch, confesses his regressive jealousy, and works out all his problems with the help of a cheque book and vast swathes of the afternoon. All frightfully tedious, but possibly effective, if you can bear it.

But you can't, and I don't blame you. In which case, you've got to have the courage of your old-fashioned convictions. Be a Cave Man and sort yourself out, with plenty of action and attitude.

First, admit that you have behaved like an absolute heel and got what was coming to you. You have lived the life of a rake, and received a rake's reward. Tell yourself that it only serves you right, and you are going to take your punishment like a man.

Next, face your anger. You are absolutely livid that other men got there before you – and why shouldn't you be? You feel furious and humiliated. The traditional place to off-load these feelings is on the rugby pitch. Take up some extremely unpleasant and aggressive sport, and thrash out your rage by beating up a few other Cave Men within the rules of the game. Winning from time to time will help restore your macho image to yourself.

And avoid your lady for a while. Allow yourself an evening of being a New Man to explain this to her courteously: you don't want to hurt or upset her, and you certainly don't want to lose her. So tell her that you need some time alone and you will be back when you've pulled yourself together. (And ask her, please, on no account to have an affair with someone else while you are away ...)

If none of this works, there's nothing wrong with getting medical help with impotence: it isn't really therapy in the loony sense of the word. But my hunch is, if you follow this course of action rigorously enough, your sex drive will return in its own good time.

And I suggest you and your true love decide to be faithful to each other from now on. A little device that many find helpful is a wedding ring.

DEAR ANNE – Is there such a thing as conjugal rights? After 25 years of marriage, I just want to be left in peace. Sex is over-rated and only necessary for procreation; my husband's advances feel like a violation and I think he should be satisfied with other demonstrations of affection. But he says he feels cheated of his rights. Are we doomed?
A wife and mother, London

That depends on you. Of course conjugal rights exist. Husband and wife owe them to each other. You say you love your husband, but you are refusing to give him the affection he needs. It is particularly distressing that you talk of violation. You chose to give yourself to him 25 years ago. Why does this now feel like rape?

The problem is not really about sex, but about other issues in your relationship. You are depriving your husband of something that does indeed belong to him: you yourself. Tell him you want to love him better, but explain that you can't change overnight and you will need to work on the problem together. Then get help. Start with your GP, who can refer you to a sex therapist; or try Relate 0845 456 1310 (www.relate.org.uk). But whatever you do, don't patronize him or think of yourself as a martyr. The only thing more miserable than not having sex with your spouse is being made to feel he or she is doing you a favour.

DEAR ANNE – I strongly disagree with your views on 'conjugal rights'. Sex in marriage is not a right, but a privilege. Only a cad would insist on such 'rights'.

Nor do I agree with your proposition that, as long as the couple concerned is legally married, 'anything goes' as far as sex is concerned. To judge from some of your replies, you seem to think that a woman should behave like a nun before the wedding, and a prostitute afterwards!

Mrs J.A.B., Surrey

Yes, I think that sums up the Christian attitude to sex pretty neatly; all I would add is that men should behave in the same way.

I agree that only a cad would demand these rights in an unloving way; but only a cad would deny them, too.

St Paul said that a married person has no authority over his body; he owes it to his spouse to make love frequently (1 Corinthians 7:5). Which just goes to show that obedience to God can be jolly good fun.

And there is sexual harassment:

DEAR ANNE – A senior colleague takes a keen interest in me and keeps inviting me out for lunch. Since I have ambitions to work in his area of expertise, and I need his recommendation to change departments, I am anxious not to offend him. My problem is that I fear his interest in me is romantic rather than professional. I have tried all the old tricks – including bringing up my fiancé in conversation – but this has not put him off. How can I stay on friendly terms with him without encouraging his amorous intentions?

D.R., Windermere

By being ruthlessly businesslike: accept only necessary lunch invitations; don't drink when you're out with him; make sure you always have 2 p.m. appointments afterwards; avoid late dinners, or business trips together. If he starts harassing you, you can report him, but it sounds as though his attentions are perfectly correct, if unwelcome.

And, as in any tricky situation, humour often diverts disaster. One secretary had a boss who kept calling her 'Darling' whenever they were in public together. He stopped the day she retaliated: 'Yes, Daddy?'

DEAR ANNE – For the last few months, I have regularly been receiving 'dirty' telephone calls at home. They aren't serious enough yet for me to change my number or go ex-directory; and I don't particularly want to screen them through my answerphone, because my friends then think I'm out and hang up. But these calls always leave me feeling upset and angry, and I spend half the evening trying to forget about them. Is there anything else I could do?
Name and address supplied

Yes. Pretend to be slightly deaf. Ask the caller to repeat himself a little louder because you couldn't quite catch what he said. Then do it again. And again. By the time he has repeated the same obscenity a dozen times, no longer in a hoarse whisper but in a desperate shout, he will feel a complete ninny. The loser is the one who hangs up first: on no account should this be you. When you finally suggest it might be easier for him to talk to your husband (or boyfriend) since he has much better hearing, and besides he is a vicar (or policeman, sex-therapist, whatever) so he should be able to help, the heavy breather will end the call in some consternation and the most acute embarrassment – and you will laugh all night long.

DEAR ANNE – I am worried about my husband's new acquaintance. He rang the other day, and, when he realized my husband was out, asked me whether I was wearing sexy underwear. I was incensed, but my husband merely found it funny. What should I say next time I see him?
S. Jones, Merseyside

Try: 'Is that a mobile telephone in your pocket? I wish I had one that small.'

2. Who Should I Be Suing?

Plenty of people complained, not just *about* my column, but to it and in it as well.

DEAR ANNE – Ever growing crowds at seaside resorts in summer are making things even worse for disabled people. My husband and I both have serious cancer, are not as nimble as we used to be and cannot 'dodge' skates or boards. We have to shop, so we try to choose non-busy hours – but Eastbourne always seems to be packed with students.
Marian Ward, Bexhill

Shopping brings me out in a dreadful temper, so I never do it now: I buy clothes from a catalogue (or, more often, pinch my daughters') and order everything else by telephone. I also hate choosing food; I have asked our greengrocer to deliver anything he likes, every Saturday. If we don't recognize something, we try it out on the chickens first. John Lewis shops deliver everything free (even a bar of kitchen soap) to within 30 miles. Unfortunately, there isn't a branch near you and I couldn't find anything similar, but you can do supermarket shopping by internet or, if you're not online, by telephone in most areas.

Meanwhile, you do still need to take exercise, so may I suggest the following: a very loud bicycle horn; a walking stick; large, beefy grandsons; a yappy dog; one of those squirty things for misting plants/spraying students; a son-in-law in the police force. Hope one of these helps.

DEAR ANNE – I couldn't believe your sarcastic, self-congratulatory reply to the lady from Bexhill who finds shopping hard. Your replies have often angered or saddened me, but this one takes the biscuit. Do you ever consider human frailty when you are faced with helplessness or despair, or have these emotions never touched your perfect life? Since the woman in question lives near the coast, I was surprised that you didn't suggest that she emulates you and walks on water. An apology is in order.
Eva Jones, Leamington Spa

DEAR ANNE – Thank you for your reply to our letter about shopping. It was very enjoyable, but it hasn't solved the problem. We live in a remote village, all our friends are old and there are no delivery services or local shops around here any more. We are badly incapacitated by cancer and both in our eighties, so we do find it hard to get around.
Marian Ward, Cooden, Bexhill

The proper, long-term answer is for the rest of us to complain vigorously and continually to our MPs about our increasingly motorized society, and get out of our cars and start using buses, trains, feet and village shops. However, that won't help you immediately and I would hate Eva Jones to waste another stamp. Your Care At Home Services (01424 848088) will do your shopping for you, but they charge £11.30 an hour. Social Services (0845 601 0664) will provide home help after a financial assessment (the duty officer was full of good ideas, so it's worth talking to them anyway) and you may qualify for an attendance allowance from the DSS (01424 452000). Another useful number is Bexhill Caring Community (01424 215116), who help with shopping, and Age Concern (01424 215674). The Co-op, near you (01424 844744), says it stocks most essentials and there is a taxi service next door to them; the journey from your house will set you back about £5. Best of all is Helping Hands, which runs a free delivery service (01424 732700). It is happy to call on you every week. You can ring up and order your groceries, fruit and vegetables beforehand, or decide what to buy when it calls. Happy shopping.

I loved this next. As complaints went, I thought, it was seriously imaginative.

DEAR ANNE – The other day, at work, I received a huge and hideous bouquet from my boyfriend – gladdies, gypsophilia, chrysanthemums, even carnations. I was so embarrassed. Every other girl in my office is treated to tasteful, co-ordinated displays from Harper & Tom's. How can I tell him that Interflora is not where it's at?
Sophia Balfour, Chelsea

Give him my address. Dandelions, cow parsley, I don't care…

DEAR ANNE – Please tell Sophia Balfour, who received a 'huge and hideous bouquet' from her boyfriend, to grow up.
Gill Jeffrey, Hemel Hempstead

DEAR ANNE – What an insufferably spoilt snob Sophia must be.
Wendy Charles-Warner, Salisbury.

And the next seems to be quite a common one, most depressingly. (Surely the *Telegraph* is supposed to be read by chivalrous, old-fashioned chaps?)

DEAR ANNE – When my boyfriend and I go to the pub, he gallantly rushes to the bar. He always returns with a pint of Guinness for him and a diet Coke for me – and hands me his car keys. I am tiring of this unspoken 'arrangement'. What can I do?
J.S., Barnes

Next time you drive him home, as you turn slowly out into the road past the pub's brick wall, I suggest you take the corner just a tiny little bit too tightly.

DEAR ANNE – When we go to parties, my husband always drinks too much to drive home. I think this is unfair, as it means that I can never relax and enjoy myself. What can I do?
S.B., Cambridgeshire

Since you live in Cambridgeshire, I'm amazed you even ask. Go by bike, of course. I've frequently been drunk in charge of a bicycle, but I've never yet been arrested – or not for that, anyway.

DEAR ANNE – I was absolutely appalled to read that you ride a bicycle when under the influence of alcohol. Cyclists are dangerous enough already. No doubt you'll be telling us next that you ride through red lights, go up on the pavement, and charge about without a helmet.
A disgusted motorist

As it happens, I do – all three, though the former usually only late at night, on deserted roads (deserted by policemen, anyway). But I've never yet endangered any life other than my own, from my bicycle.

The difference is that drunken cyclists don't kill people; even sober drivers kill several people a day.

DEAR ANNE – Being 37 weeks pregnant, I am beginning to find it difficult to move around. But though my condition is now obvious, I am surprised at how few people offer me a seat when I am on packed buses or the Tube. Those who have done so – and there have not been many – were predominantly young women. And the only man who showed me this courtesy was also young. It does shock me to see middle-aged, middle-class men – including *Telegraph* readers – ignoring elderly people and those struggling with young children. My husband tells me that many men are not chivalrous any more because they are worried that women who see such gestures as 'chauvinistic' will react angrily. What do you think?
Dora Warren, London EC1

Dear, oh dear. What are you, men or mice, you weedy male *Telegraph* readers out there? Let's have a show of solidarity, please. In future, seats in the Tube should be given up to the elderly, of either sex. Men should stand up so women can sit, and parents carrying children – in or out of the womb – are to be looked after by the rest of us. *Of course* a pregnant woman must always be given space and a seat – although a man may also offer her a knee if he is very strong (and not too knobbly). And chaps, if an annoyed feminist punches you on the nose, I suggest you spank her bottom. (I might even organize a column whip-round for your law suit.) So no more slobbing about without manners – particularly not if you are openly reading this paper. If you

A pregnant woman must also be given space.

see a fellow *Telegraph* reader behaving disgracefully, roll up your copy and thwack him one. And then we'll all club together and buy him a subscription to the *Guardian*.

DEAR ANNE – Regarding giving seats to the elderly on the London Underground: a few weeks ago, I was travelling with my mother, who suffers from arthritis and angina and is in her late eighties. We stepped on to a crowded Victoria line train, and, since no one volunteered, I said in a clear voice: 'Will someone please give my mother a seat?'

A deathly hush followed until finally, reluctantly, a young man rose to his feet. Recounting this episode to my brother, I said I didn't know what I would have done if no one had responded.

'Well,' he replied, 'you could have shouted: "If none of you is going to stand up, five of you clear your laps so that she can lie down!"'

Mrs Elizabeth MacLeod, Middlesex

DEAR ANNE – Re: the whining letter from your pregnant correspondent, who was silly enough to expect men to stand up for her on the Tube. You can't slice it both ways: it's no good you women insisting on your right to be equal in the nice things – such as salaries – without expecting to have to open your own doors and carry your shopping.

B.H.G., South London (address withheld because – poor wimp – he says he is frightened of a brick through his window)

Well, some idiot had to say it. I realize it is a difficult concept for you, but being equal does not mean being identical. What do you do if a disabled person needs help crossing the road? Tell him to pull himself together and get on with it, if he claims entitlement to the same pay at work? And how do you suggest we achieve equality in bearing children? Are you volunteering yourself for pregnancy? Men can't do much for their unborn children, but women recognize it isn't your fault and give you an equal stake in bringing them up. Civilized people consider it a privilege to care for the next generation, and are pleased to show consideration – and gratitude – towards pregnant mothers.

If you haven't got a brain, don't try to use it: I'm sure some kind woman will think your next thoughts for you.

But he was sadly not alone. A few men seem to find it remarkably hard to understand the principle of equality within diversity …

DEAR ANNE – Often, when I travel by Tube I give up my seat to elderly fellow passengers. But I am getting fed up of doing this while men remain seated around me. Have you any suggestions?
Alice, Chiswick

Try saying, rather loudly: 'As there are no gentlemen to give you their seat, would you like mine?'

DEAR ANNE – With regard to Alice of Chiswick wondering why men no longer give up their seats on trains, the corollary of sexual equality means that it can no longer be the case that a gentleman must offer his seat to a lady. Women and men are either equals or not. Women cannot expect to have it both ways.
Andrew Wauchope, Kennington

Why on earth not?

I have never known any other agony aunt receive so many responses to her responses. By the law of averages, some of the comments were bound to be complaints. (Does this say more about me, or my readership?)

DEAR ANNE – I am a chartered surveyor. My wife and I have, until now, led a happy and conventional life. We have a son of 27 and a daughter of 25, both of whom have flown the nest.

However, my wife has announced that she wants a mountain bike for her 54th birthday next week, and she also wants to go to the Glastonbury Festival next year. Not long ago, she tried to go to an Elton John concert at Wembley, but could not get a ticket.

Please can you advise me on how to persuade her to grow old gracefully?
H.R., Dorking

Certainly not. She is ageing very gracefully already. What is the matter with you? It sounds as if you think that age is an excuse to become fat, lazy and set in your ways, while your wife exercises her body and mind. How are you going to cope when you can't play football with your grandchildren without getting out of breath?

Wake up. Your wife is only in her fifties. If you want an example of what it means to be 50, look at Goldie Hawn.

My parents are in their eighties: my father is as fit as a fiddle because he bicycles everywhere, and my mother has just taken on two dozen new maths pupils.

So buy your wife that mountain bike and get one for yourself, too – otherwise she might pedal over the horizon and leave you far behind.

DEAR ANNE – After your reply to H.R. (column, 3 July), I really feel obliged to write and tell you that you owe your readers more respect. You are too keen to tell people to 'pull themselves together' and 'wake up'. Is it really necessary to be so brusque?
Richard Snead-Cox,
London SW6

No, you're right. I apologize, and will try to do better. Meanwhile, may I very respectfully advise you to grow up and get a life.

Happily, both correspondents recently updated me on HR's agonizing dilemma, which clearly troubled all three of us so deeply.

The mountain bike arrived, and is still used to exercise the Labradors. This year we have both celebrated our 60th birthdays, and also our 35th Wedding Anniversary, so she has not, yet, pedalled over the horizon nor (perish the thought) gone to the Glastonbury Festival.

Incidentally, I telephoned Mr Snead-Cox, who had taken my letter and your reply so much to heart…
Hugh Richards, Dorking

I gave *you* advice, but you didn't take to it kindly – unusual, I know. Afterwards, a man rang me from Esher and suggested I attend to your advice.

You told me to get a life and grow up. I have done just that, and am a better person for it.
J. Richard Snead-Cox

DEAR ANNE – I am at a highly academic girls' school, and returned from holiday to find that most of my class had got straight A*s in their GCSEs. How can I be happy with my (OK) grades when all my friends are so disgustingly brilliant?
A.C. (aged 16), Edgware

You're a national heroine. Everyone worries about grades going up, which suggests that standards are going down. But you have single-handedly redressed the balance. The academic reputation of the entire educational system rests on your slender shoulders. Walk tall.

"Yes, I've failed politics!"

DEAR ANNE – I was sickened by your frivolous response to A.C. (3 September) about her GCSE grades not being good enough. We cracked open the champagne when my son got his six A–C grades, which enabled him to take up his place at sixth-form college. I thought you were in the business of giving responsible advice.
Name and address withheld

How very kind of you: I don't think anyone's ever said that to me before. Regular readers often honour me with brief, amusing difficulties, like the one last week, in which the correspondent complained (playfully) that her school friends were 'disgustingly brilliant'. One of the best ways of coping with problems is to laugh about them: if others want to make light of their shortcomings, who are you to criticize?

Thanks to our exam system and the Special Needs of one of our children, I have experienced quite enough heartache to know how important and – far more crucially – unimportant exams can be. Your son has his health, his future and a loving family who can afford to celebrate his success with champagne. What are you complaining about?

Not all the complaints were about me, happily.

DEAR ANNE – My washing machine has broken down. First, the engineer didn't turn up when he said he would, so I waited in all day. Then I asked him to come before I left for work, and he arrived so early that he got me out of bed. When I got home, I discovered he had 'fixed' the dishwasher, which was already in perfect working order. He now wants to be paid. What do you suggest?
H. Greenwood, Chiswick

Tell him that the cheque is in the post – sent to an engineer by another name, at a different address.

DEAR ANNE – I have just received the following anonymous chain letter: 'You will receive luck within four days of receiving this provided that you send it out. This is no joke. Send copies to people you think need good luck. Do not keep this letter. It must leave your hands within 96 hours. John received £40,000 and lost it because he broke the chain. Gene lost his wife after receiving the letter: he failed to circulate it. Helen received the letter and did nothing with it and died nine days later. Do not ignore this. For some strange reason, it works.' I don't like the tone of this – what should I do?
R.J., Staffordshire

I can tell you exactly what to do, because I received the very same letter myself. It should indeed leave your hands immediately – though preferably within 96 seconds rather than hours. Put it in the waste paper basket and it will bring you instant good luck: it will save you time, save you a stamp and save you looking a fool. Trust me. It works.

DEAR ANNE – We live in a small street and our neighbours have taken to bagging a parking space by leaving bins outside their house. This makes the situation very difficult for the rest of us. How can we retaliate?
C.H., London

Move them. Then fill them with cement.

DEAR ANNE – Following your impressive reply to the reader with awful neighbours (5 November), I enclose a photograph of my neighbour's house. He has not painted it for 27 years and the exterior has turned an eerie black. He is an absentee owner and ignores our letters. Any suggestions?
T.C., Holt

He lives in a house like Hermann Munster's, and he's absent? Make a forced entry, make up a ghost story, make a fortune conducting tours around his haunted house … then move to a stately home where you won't have any neighbours.

DEAR ANNE – My new cleaner, whom I like, has left an iron-shaped burn in the middle of my sitting room carpet. What should I do?
D.T., Chelsea

Don't make a mountain out of a molehill. Move house.

DEAR ANNE – I have a problem. I am a boring, balding, white, male, middle-class commuter, who would like to become an exciting, black, lesbian, one-legged, culturally plural, New-Agey chattering-class wimmin with big hair. Auntie Anne, who should I be suing?
David Pickering, Tooting

The teacher who didn't tell you when to use the accusative of the interrogative pronoun. You mean whom, not who.

DEAR ANNE – Fortunately, I'm between problems at the moment, so I'm just writing to say how much I appreciate your column.
A.J. Jones, Wembley

DEAR ANNE – Help! Your column is becoming clogged up with readers' feedback. I don't know what to do. I want more problems!
John Boas, Bath

3. Don't Even Say Goodbye

Whenever people asked me what agony featured more often than anything else, I replied that by far the most popular problem seemed to be adultery. This could, of course, reflect the readership of the *Daily Telegraph* … but I suspect, glancing at my Old Testament, it represents human frailty more generally.

Adultery was, after all, the reason the agony column was invented.

Early in 1691 John Dunton, a 32-year-old printer and bookseller, was strolling with friends in St George's Fields, Lambeth. His mind was troubled. He was conducting an extra-marital affair, and longed to confide in somebody. He thought of unburdening his soul to a clergyman, but more even than the relief of confession, he wanted the security of anonymity: 'how to conceal myself and the wretch was the difficulty'.

Suddenly it struck him. If he had this need, others must have it too. Perhaps he could turn his sin to profit. He turned to his companions and said, 'Well, Sirs, I have a thought I will not exchange for fifty guineas.' His brainwave was to have a publication to which readers could write with questions, which were then published and answered together.

On 10 March 1691, *The Athenian Gazette* (soon *The Athenian Mercury*) was launched. The name was, of course, taken from Acts 17:21, 'For all the Athenians and strangers which were there spent their time in nothing else, but either to tell, or to hear some new thing.'

To help him answer the questions, Dunton recruited the mathematician Richard Sault, and his future brother-in-law, Samuel Wesley (father of Charles and John). And true to its Athenian precedent, the majority of questions in the *Gazette* were far broader than the readers' own personal egocentric worries about love or sex: Creation, slave-trading, perpetual motion and why an hour's sermon seems longer than two hours' conversation – all the kind of queries that I loved to include too.

But adultery was the agony that sparked it all off.

DEAR ANNE – Since the age of four, Sophie and I have been best friends; we went to the same schools and shared a house at university. Naturally, we have come to regard each other's families as extended versions of our own. Six months ago, I visited her parents. Her mother was out, so I sat down to talk to her father. He is a retired Army officer and has many interesting stories. We were soon on to our second bottle of wine and having a very jolly time. When I went to get some nibbles out of a top cupboard, I felt his hand on my bottom. To my surprise, I responded positively to his advances and we have been having an affair ever since. I really love him, but I don't want to hurt Sophie, or her mother, who will be seventy-two next week.
B.K., Oxon

What advice do you want? How to have your cake and eat it? Or how to keep your lover without losing your friend and devastating her mother? It can't be done. Adultery hurts. You have to choose between the friend you've had all your life and your lover of six months – who didn't strike you as your one and only soul-mate until he touched your bottom.

If you seriously want my advice, here it is: put as much distance between Sophie's father and yourself as possible. Don't see him again until you are over him. And then, don't see him alone. Ever. Finally, find yourself a man who isn't a cheat.

DEAR ANNE – A few weeks ago, you dismissed an elderly married man, having an affair with a younger woman, as a 'cheat'. I am elderly and have been married for over 30 years to an attractive woman. However, her indifference and then aversion to any sexual activity between us led to its decline and ultimate non-existence. After a lifetime of fidelity and unhappy celibacy, I have recently been having an affair with a slightly younger woman which has given us great pleasure, and fulfilment.

　　Am I a cheat?
B.T., London

Of course. You were asked whether you would 'keep thee only unto her, so long as ye both shall live.' You took the promise voluntarily. Now, you are breaking it – repeatedly and deliberately. What do you call that? And what did you have in mind when you said you took her 'for better for worse'?

DEAR ANNE – Two weeks ago, you dismissed as a cheat a man who, after years of enforced celibacy, had found a measure of happiness outside his marriage. I feel your judgment was wrong and deeply unkind. Please imagine the rejection, increasing unkindness, insults – obscenity even – suffered over many years by the loving spouse. My three-year-old son has never seen his father touch me or kiss me. And he will never have a sibling, because my husband won't sleep with me.

P., South Wales

DEAR ANNE – Your reply to this obviously lonely man absolutely stinks.

Miss L. Charles, Huntingdon, Cambridgeshire

DEAR ANNE – This is to protest at your reply to B.T., the 'cheating husband'. His wife has long since broken her vows to love, honour and cherish him.

D. M. Digby, London NW10

I agree. But she didn't write to me. If she had, I would have told her that she is a cheat too – and that she should stop being so selfish, rip off her clothes and jump into bed with him straight away. And P. from South Wales (above) also has a husband who is cheating on her, by refusing to make love to her: he is breaking his vows as surely as, and perhaps far more cruelly than, B.T. But P.'s problems will not necessarily be solved if she cheats as well and takes a lover. Our wedding vows are not conditional. We don't promise to 'love, honour and cherish provided you always do this to me'. If we did, we could all walk out of our marriages the following week, since no one ever loves or cherishes his spouse enough.

If you re-read B.T.'s question more carefully, you will find that he didn't ask me for advice, or understanding. He simply asked whether, having broken his vows and embarked on an extra-marital affair, he was cheating. If a starving man steals a loaf, he is still a thief – though we can all sympathize with him.

So I repeat my assertion. B.T. is a cheat.

DEAR ANNE – A few years ago, I became infatuated with one of my colleagues, although nothing physical took place. A year later, my wife fell in love with someone else and left me for him, taking the children with her. I am being divorced for my unreasonable behaviour. Should I feel guilty and was I a 'cheat'?

K.L., Kent

No, and no.

DEAR ANNE – My wife is six months pregnant and will not sleep with me. Recently, I have become close friends with a female colleague. At a Christmas party a few weeks ago, she revealed that she was extremely attracted to me and I spent the night with her. I am deeply confused about what to do now. Things have been awkward at work, but as far as I know, no one else knows. Should I tell my wife about what happened? I do regret my behaviour, but if my wife can't satisfy my sexual needs, I feel that this could happen again.
Name and address supplied

If you regret it, you presumably wish it hadn't taken place and would prefer that it weren't repeated. Yet you say, 'This could happen again', as if it were a clap of thunder or the collapse of the stock market: something over which you have no control. Don't be so defeatist. Take charge of your life, and don't let things 'happen' that you don't want. When you were asked at your wedding whether you would be faithful to your wife, you didn't say, 'with a bit of luck', but 'I will'. It is an effort of the will, and you need to give yourself some help. You're feeling sexually frustrated at the moment (understandably), so avoid temptation: don't go to parties, or on business trips, without your wife. Spend more time with her. Try to sympathize with what's happening to her physically, and remember the exciting reason for it. Ask yourself whether you would respect another man for embarking on fatherhood with an extramarital affair on the go.

Out of courtesy, and to help prevent a recurrence, explain your regrets to your colleague. An old-fashioned apology to her might not go amiss. It's not necessarily right to tell your wife what happened: only you, or a close friend of you both, could weigh up the pain it would cause against the benefit of being open. But you ought to tell her how frustrated you feel. Ask for her help. If she does not want intercourse at the moment – which is understandable, and is likely to be the case for a while after the baby is born – there's more than one way to skin a cat, and plenty of ways of giving a man sexual satisfaction … which I leave to your imagination. I suggest the two of you give it a free rein, and have fun.

DEAR ANNE – Ten years ago, my husband asked for a divorce because I was having an affair. He insisted on keeping the children, so they stayed with him and I lived nearby with my new man. It all worked brilliantly for a few years, until he remarried. At that point, our younger child came to live with me. He has had his fair share of trouble, so the past two years have been terribly stressful for me – exacerbated by a lack of support from his father. I admit that I have a good husband and two healthy children, no money worries and a good job. But recently, I rang my ex to share my feelings about our youngest son, and he put the phone down on me. I feel totally worthless. Is this God paying me back for my sins, or just a stubborn man wanting to get his own back? What do I have to do to be treated as a human being by the father of my children? I have tried praying and have confessed my sins many times. I don't ask for much, except that my children are happy and successful in their lives. My vicar has suggested I've only received what was coming to me.
Name and address withheld

I'm sorry to sound harsh, but I think your vicar has a point. Is God 'paying you back'? If you bought a new car and drove it over broken bottles at 70 miles an hour – in first gear with the brakes on – would you blame the maker if it didn't run well? Our Maker has given us clear instructions, and you have ignored them all: He hates divorce, dislikes broken promises and condemns adultery most of all. You have indulged in all three, and now express surprise that life isn't all hunky-dory. 'All' you want is happiness and success for your children, but you have cheated on their father, broken up their home and parted brother from brother. You have messed up three lives, and the sum total of your complaint is that someone has put the telephone down on you. I think God has been remarkably merciful.

It is good that you have confessed your sins, and when we do this our Maker forgives us. But He doesn't necessarily undo the harm we've done. King David was forgiven by God for his adultery, but God still allowed the result of his adultery to take its course and David's little baby boy to die.

I think you should apologize to your former husband (and children) as well as to God. Write, saying sorry for having the affair and breaking up the marriage. But don't necessarily expect a reply, or that your ex will ever be able to talk to you again without pain. And keep praying.

DEAR ANNE – I read last week that you do not believe in sex outside marriage. So, what happens if you are vitally heterosexual, 50, and your husband has had no interest in you sexually for the past 15 years? What if you feel your celibacy like a daily burden, and hate it beyond endurance? It is incompatible with my Christianity to take a lover – and I've had many offers – but I am overwhelmed with sadness and feel no self-esteem because there is no sex in my life. Am I justified in taking a bit of the joy that is offered before I am dead?
Name and address supplied

Even if you were justified, would an affair bring you joy? Ask yourself how much happiness such a relationship would provide, not just in the first few weeks or months (when your self-esteem probably would improve) but a year or two afterwards, or in 20 years' time. Do you simply want sex? Or do you want sex with the man you love, and all the affection and intimacy you once shared with him?

You don't say whether you have talked to your husband about it. But you must. He may be suffering from impotence, and be feeling guilty and too embarrassed to tell you. Talking about it could give him the confidence to seek medical help. Or, there may be something else wrong, which a family psychologist might help you both with. If appropriate, ask your GP to help. You can get Christian counselling from Marriage Resource 01202 849000 (www.marriageresource. org.uk). Show your husband understanding, love and the commitment you obviously have, but do not let him avoid the issue.

DEAR ANNE – We have been married for 12 years, and had difficulty having children until five years ago, when we had a beautiful daughter. However, because she is handicapped, I became quite depressed after she was born. My husband refused to talk about it or go with me for counselling, and it was a very difficult time.

Last autumn, I started a degree course and fell in love. I've been having an affair with a fellow student for six months, and I feel alive for the first time. In fact, we are all benefiting. My daughter is happier, and my husband has even agreed to counselling (I haven't told him about my lover, because I don't want to upset him).

Unfortunately, a girlfriend let me down badly by telling our vicar, who has asked to see me. (I have been a Christian for 10 years.) I know he will tell me to confess to my husband, but I don't want to risk my marriage. Can you advise me

how to prepare for this meeting and how to be assertive?
Name and address supplied

You have precious little to be assertive about. I realize you have had a difficult few years, and bringing up a handicapped child is never easy. But, believe me, it will be considerably harder if you lose your husband by having an affair.

You are making a complete fool of yourself, and are lucky to have a friend who cares enough to stop you, and a vicar principled enough to bother.

Of course adultery is fun to begin with, but to think that it is doing your family good is like believing a bottle of whisky has made you witty.

How serious are you about your faith? When Jesus was asked how we can inherit eternal life, he said: 'You know the commandments: Do not commit adultery' (Mark 10:19).

Before seeing your vicar, I suggest you get a concordance and read every biblical reference to adultery. A confession to your husband might indeed damage your marriage. But if you could promise the vicar that you have repented and will never see your lover again, I expect he would agree to your keeping silent.

Otherwise, he would be perfectly justified in denying you Communion – and your husband might want to know why.

DEAR ANNE – My GP of 12 years is a married man. Recently, I told him – and I accept this was wrong – that I wanted to start a physical relationship with him. He responded some weeks later by trying to kiss me. I don't want to put his career and marriage in jeopardy. However, he is kind and humorous and treats me considerately, and I am finding it difficult to cope with this continual sexual frustration.

You may think I should simply find another GP. But I feel I need to see him, even if our relationship remains platonic.

I think he is neither content in his marriage nor in his job, and I long to make him happy. But I was brought up to consider adultery wrong. What should I do?
Name and address supplied

You're absolutely right: I think you should change your GP. Apart from anything else, he has demonstrated extreme folly and lack of professionalism by continuing to treat you.

I dare say he is not happy in his marriage or his job: he is certainly risking both by allowing both of you to keep indulging in temptation. But you don't want the responsibility for ruining his life, so ask that your medical notes be transferred and leave at once.

If you continue your present course of action, one of two things will happen. Either you will prolong your frustration and postpone finding a more suitable and available companion, or you will start an affair with him which would indeed destroy both his career and his marriage.

Not seeing him will be hard, of course, and you will go through great pain to begin with. Soon, though, you will be able to start afresh and develop friendships that have a future.

Don't even say goodbye: just go.

4. Setting a Bad Example

The other topic that agony aunts are traditionally asked about is etiquette. And indeed, next after adultery in popularity amongst *Telegraph* readers was agony over the vexed question of thank-you letters.

DEAR ANNE – Some time ago, my husband and I received an invitation to the confirmation of the son of family friends. As we were unable to attend, I sent him a cheque for £25. Although I never received a thank-you letter, after three months, the cheque was cashed.

I always answer letters promptly, although my children tell me I am old-fashioned. But surely common courtesy cannot go out of fashion?
J.B., Ilford

You wouldn't believe the number of letters I receive on this subject. The old cannot understand how the young can be so rude.

I sympathize with both. I know invitations should be acknowledged and letters replied to, and presents deserve a proper thank you. Yet my own stack of unanswered letters is the bane of my life. I find older friends and relations often cannot imagine how insanely hectic modern life has become and how difficult it is to find time for graciousness.

Details of etiquette are culturally conditioned: clothes, forms of address, and so on change from one generation to another. But basic consideration for others is essential for any civilized society, so it is inexcusable not to thank someone for a present. But it is not unforgivable.

The boy should have written to you, but try to be generous and understanding. It doesn't mean he didn't appreciate your cheque.

DEAR ANNE – Every year I give my grandchildren their Christmas presents, but it takes them weeks to post me their thankyou letters.

How can I encourage better manners?
Mrs A.P., Exeter

Get online.

"Granny! Stop surfing the internet and get on with your 'thank you' letters!"

DEAR ANNE – After the recent death of my husband, I received more than 100 letters of condolence and a similar number of cards. I have almost finished writing 'thank-you' notes to those who wrote letters. But do I have an obligation to answer all the cards?
E.E., Chichester

You are under no obligation to write to anyone. Your friends and acquaintances wrote to you to express their love, concern and sympathy; I am sure most of them would be dismayed if they thought they had put a burden upon you.

It is lovely that you have written so many replies already, and if you can drop very brief notes to those who sent cards, they will certainly be well-received and appreciated. (What some people do is get a card printed, apologizing for not being able to write personally.)

But be kind to yourself. Writing letters should be a pleasure. If you can't face the thought of doing so – or can't afford the time or stamps – don't worry. Only an exceptionally mean-minded person would resent a recently widowed friend neglecting such a task.

DEAR ANNE – I like Christmas but I dont like riting thank you letters. do I haf to
Daisy Jones Age 5.

Yup.

Dear, oh dear. Daisy wasn't very satisfied with my letter, I'm afraid – or indeed the edited version of hers.

Most of the correspondence sent to me had to be cut: after all, some of it went on for pages. Much also had to be clarified: when you are in the throes of life's agonies, you can't always express your problems simply. And troubles seldom come singly, so correspondents would sometimes want to describe all the difficulties that had led to the present one: the skill lay in boiling the letter down to what was bothering its writer most, and what most needed changing. So most letters were edited. The exceptions were the short, amusing ones, which were usually published exactly as they were received.

But the point is that a certain amount of licence was needed before the letters could be reproduced. I never received any objections … until Daisy's.

Her original had in fact been this:

DEAR ANNE – I like Christmas, but I dont like riting thank you letters. wat do I do
Daisy Jones Age 5.

To which, of course, I should have replied,

Write them anyway.

But my edited version enabled my reply to be briefer, snappier, and made the same point. I thought.

Daisy's (absolutely valid) objection was that she knew she had to write them: of course she did. She was a very correctly brought up young lady. There was no question in her mind as to whether or not she should do so. But she had wanted to know what to do about not liking the task.

As far as I remember, my letter of explanation and apology ran to several large handwritten page. A friend, who saw the sheaves of explanation sprawling over my desk, said it's no wonder I never get to the bottom of my correspondence.

DEAR ANNE – When my daughters asked Daisy Jones's question ('I don't like riting thank you letters. do I haf to?'), I replied: No problem. Just give me the gifts and I'll send them back. Needless to say, I've had no problems since.
G. Batchelor, Daventry

We had a Canadian au pair whose mother actually did this one year. Her daughter certainly never forgot the lesson. But it does strike me as a rather bizarre way of teaching children gratitude, since it is surely even ruder to all the kind uncles and aunts who have taken the trouble to choose the lovely presents in the first place...

DEAR ANNE – With reference to your New Year correspondence about thank-you letters, I have become persona non grata with my husband's family. We decided, jointly, not to send Christmas presents to his sister's children, aged eleven, eight and four, as we never received any acknowledgment of the birthday presents we had sent them during the year. My sister-in-law rang up after Christmas and asked me whether I had sent anything for her children. When I explained why I hadn't, she told me I was mean, despicable and didn't understand how their family worked. Now my parents-in-law have become involved. They say it is not my business to moralize, which has put my husband in a difficult position. I always insist on my children writing thank-you letters, which they now do willingly. Everyone else I know expects the same of their children.
Name and address supplied

This is a tricky situation. You have undoubtedly been wronged. Presents are freely given, so it is outrageous to suggest that anyone is obliged to provide them. If you can't afford them, didn't have time to shop, or, as in this case, don't like giving presents to people who

Setting a Bad Example **49**

don't say thank you, that is no one else's business. For your sister-in-law to call and demand presents (rather than simply check whether they got lost in the post) is monstrous.

However, your parents-in-law are right about one thing (which is good news, because it will help considerably if you have something to concede): it isn't your job to bring up your sister-in-law's children. Have you interfered, or been judgmental? Look back over the events, and try to find something for which you can apologize, even if it was just a word of irritation or a tactless turn of phrase. This will help to defuse the situation, and help your husband, too. After all, it is largely up to him to bring about a reconciliation, while remaining loyal to you. Ask him to take responsibility for your joint decision. Then go along with him, however he decides to mend the bridges, even if it means swallowing your pride. And make it clear to your children that your standards of letter-writing still apply, whatever the rules in another family.

DEAR ANNE – I hosted a house-warming party last week. Many of my friends brought presents, which included a fair number of bottles. Do these require thank-you letters?
Claire James, London SW3

Presents for your new house and garden, or yourself, do require thank-you letters. Contributions to the evening's entertainment, however, generally don't: an appreciative thank you at the time is enough.

I would say pot plants and fine wine that you put aside are proper presents for which you should send a brief note of thanks afterwards. Cut flowers and plonk are enjoyed on the night itself and gone with the morning – as is any need for further acknowledgment.

DEAR ANNE – We were married six weeks ago, and are just finishing our thank-you letters. However, there are a few generous friends from whom we have apparently received nothing. The postal service in our part of London is appalling, so it is possible that parcels have got lost. We don't wish to appear ungrateful for presents which may have failed to arrive, nor grasping for presents if friends have chosen not to give them. What do we do?
Name and address supplied

This is a very real problem. Miraculously, from more than 300 guests at our wedding, we only received one present that had no clear label on it. As it was of German make, we briefly wondered whether it might be from a student friend of ours who had recently lived in Germany and who hadn't given us anything else – but we thought it was far too expensive for him to have afforded, so in the end, because we didn't know what to do, we did nothing. About five years later, he made a comment that suggested he was really hurt not to have had his present acknowledged. (And it was a wonderful gift, which we are still using.) So whatever you do, do something.

Here are some suggestions: write an apologetic, rather embarrassed note to each couple from whom you have apparently received nothing, saying you were given a lovely flan dish with no name attached (bound to be true) and was it from them? Or: get someone else to snoop for you, such as the bride's mother, who could ring up (if she knows those involved) and explain your dilemma in a tactful way, asking whether you should be thanking them for anything. Or: write to everyone who hasn't sent a present, thanking them simply for being there and helping to make your wedding such a special occasion: if they are sensitive, they will get the hint and ask whether Peter Jones has delivered the electronic haggis peeler; if they are not, they will assume you have sort of thanked them anyway.

I received a delightful update to this next wedding dilemma:

DEAR ANNE – An old friend is getting married in Hong Kong. I have been told that, out of a list of 300 possible guests (among whom I was one), only 150 are being invited. Sadly, I am not among them. Have you any subtle ideas as to what I can do which would result in the bride and groom moving my name from the 'no' list to the 'yes' list, without having to send them a new Ferrari as a wedding present?
Paul, Hampshire

You could say: 'What a coincidence! I'll be in Hong Kong that very day, so can I pop in to the service?' (Anyone can attend the ceremony of a wedding; it's only the reception that requires an invitation.) Or you could ask someone on the 'yes' list to drop the couple a hint about your feelings. Or simply come clean and confess you'd love to be there, but will quite understand if there isn't room. Or just feel jolly grateful that you haven't wasted the price of a flight to Hong Kong on friends who don't really care for you.

However, the simplest and most effective of all would be to make sure they see today's *Daily Telegraph* – there can't be that many Pauls from Hampshire on their 'no' list.

This is what then happened:

> I took your advice and duly sent an anonymous copy of your column to the bride with the item outlined in red. Two days later, long before my note could have been delivered in Hong Kong much less a reply sent back, an invitation arrived. I had been on the 'yes' list all the time. Meanwhile a copy of your column was already on its way to Hong Kong. About a week later I got a phone-call from the bride in gales of laughter saying that it was the first time she had been the subject of a letter to an 'agony aunt'.
>
> The end of the story was that my wife and I went out to Hong Kong and attended the wedding and the wonderful party which followed. It was a great day. I am still in touch with the 'bride' who has two fine children and a happy marriage so all's well that ends well.
>
> I hope you include my story in your book and publish in time for Christmas. It will solve at least one Christmas present problem for me.
> Paul Corser, Hampshire

For some reason, weddings seem to bring people out in a rash of etiquamania.

DEAR ANNE – My daughter is getting married in the New Year and has planned a traditional wedding, with all the family on the top table. Unfortunately, her future in-laws are no longer on speaking terms with each other. They had an acrimonious divorce, followed by several remarriages. My daughter feels she cannot sit them down at the same table without risking unpleasantness, and is now thinking she should let people sit wherever they like. It seems such a shame. What do you think?
Name and address supplied

Under the heading 'Parental Marital Complexities', Debrett's *New Guide to Etiquette and Modern Manners* says: 'The wedding day belongs to the bride, and thus her wishes are paramount.'

Tell her to go with her original plans. If she follows the traditional seating arrangement (bride and groom in the middle, flanked by her parents, then his), her future in-laws will be nowhere near each other. And you and your husband can keep an eye on them and prevent any trouble.

You might also suggest that the groom has a word with his mother and father before the wedding: he should ask them to behave themselves, for his future wife's sake.

I had always thought the point of etiquette was to help us out when we don't know what to do, not make us feel we don't know what to do when we don't need any helping out anyway.

Some friendly advice is about as helpful as a hole in the head.

DEAR ANNE – I have recently moved to a bigger house and look forward to entertaining guests on a regular basis. However, a friend has told me to keep a book of whom I invite, and note down when they return the invitation. This all sounds rather complicated and I feel rather out of my depth. Can you recommend some guidelines?
Sophie, London SW5

The whole idea sounds utterly ghastly. Entertaining is meant to be fun, and hospitality should be generous. Do you really only want to ask people who are going to 'pay you back', or do you wish to invite those friends you want to spend an evening with or do a kindness to? Some of your friends may never be able to return the compliment, but if you appreciate their company, what does it matter? The only entertaining account I've ever heard of worth keeping is a note of what food you've served to whom (and possibly what you wore) so you don't repeat it next time – but even this is pretty frightening, and quite unnecessary.

I suggest you ignore your friend's advice. Except when you invite her.

There were some dilemmas that were very *'Telegraph'*. Somehow, I can't quite imagine this agony appearing in the *Guardian* or the *Sun*.

DEAR ANNE – Our daughter recently brought a new boyfriend home. He was a pleasant enough lad, but immediately started addressing my wife and myself by our first names. He even abbreviated mine to Andy, which I have never been called in my life. I wanted to tell him not to be so rude, but thought it might upset my daughter. Please tell me how we should cope with such appalling manners.
Andrew Jones, Teignmouth

With a little bit more charity and understanding. If you had indeed told him off, you would have been guilty of a genuine, and frightful, breach of manners – indeed of quite deliberate unkindness – whereas his only crime is ignorance about the ways of a different

"Wotcher Andy, get the kettle on old chap!"

ought to know better than to use personal names, there is not much point in taking offence at a young man who is probably anxious to impress, nervous about meeting his girlfriend's parents, and almost certainly just trying to be friendly.

Different forms of address are appropriate for different circumstances: all the children in our church address the adults by their Christian names, but with their teachers they are more formal. Children should always start by using adults' titles until they are told otherwise, but almost all of my friends prefer to be called by their first names, even by quite young children.

If you really can't cope with it, I suggest you tell your daughter to tip her boyfriend off. But it would be better for your relationships, and easier for both her and him – and therefore a sign of better manners on your part – if you could come to terms with the current situation, and accept that no slight is intended.

generation. Such over-familiarity is not so much rudeness, as a change of fashion.

Jane Austen's characters addressed even intimate friends by their surnames, a formality we would find absurd; but Chaucer's contemporaries used personal names more freely than we do. Custom has changed considerably and rapidly in recent years. Whereas professionals – nurses, doctors, insurance salesmen –

DEAR ANNE – With reference to Mr Jones's letter last week about the younger generation abandoning the use of Mr and Mrs, I was reminded of an occasion about 30 years ago, when my husband was headmaster of a prep school. One day, a small pupil came to our door asking for him by his Christian name. The child obviously didn't mean to be cheeky, so I asked him why he had chosen that form of address. He considered carefully, then said: 'I thought you would feel more comfortable.'

Perhaps Mr Jones's daughter's boyfriend thought the same? C.M.B., Cambridge

Funnily enough, this last letter was sent to my column by my mother. Well, all right, she probably scribbled it on the back of an envelope and passed it over the kitchen table one day. It's still an authentic letter, isn't it? Oh, fair enough: perhaps she did describe the event to me over the telephone. Want to make an issue of it?

She has far too much sense to be offended by someone genuinely putting himself out to make another person feel at home – especially if he is only seven.

DEAR ANNE – I feel really embarrassed to ask such a trivial question, but could you tell me how to address an envelope to my son at school. Should it be 'Master' or 'Mr'?
Mrs J.B., Taunton

Don't apologize: I'm glad it isn't more serious. At junior or prep school, he is Master Joe Bloggs. At secondary or public school, simply Joe Bloggs. Thereafter, Joe Bloggs Esq.

I got a flurry of letters telling me it was wickedly cruel to address a prep school boy as 'Master'. He would be mercilessly teased. Not to mention that old chestnut about not addressing someone as Esq. unless he owns land.

Absolute nonsense. It was my mother who taught me how to address an envelope correctly – as she taught me all the etiquette I know apart from how much to tip the beaters on a pheasant shoot (but that's all right because Holland and Holland made me mug up on this when they invited me on one) – and as the previous letter shows, her manners are infallible.

As eny fule kno, a gentleman is an Esq and a tradesman a Mr, which has nothing whatsoever to do with land. After all, almost the only people left who don't own property are clergy, who are surely still gentle if anyone is: whereas plumbers are soon going to own more of the country than the Church of England and Trinity College, Cambridge put together.

And I always addressed my sons as 'Master' when they were away at prep school. I confess, Benjamin did eventually beg me to stop writing to him. I expect he was too busy, what with Latin parsing and so on, to attend to any correspondence. I used to send him lovely postcards of fluffy little animals, with friendly messages on the back in big writing, such as, 'Lots and lots of love to my Bunnykins from Mummykins miss you all the time see you at the weekend love you xxxxx'.

It must have been a real wrench for him to stop getting these missives so he could concentrate on his studies.

DEAR ANNE – You recently advised someone how to address an envelope to her son. Please, oh please, tell us how to address our daughters. Miss, Mrs, or the dreaded Ms? Tom Underwood, Leigh-on-Sea

There is no correct way to address women any more. Whatever you do will offend. Personally, I like to be Miss when I am working, but Mrs followed by my husband's Christian name when addressed socially: 'Mrs *Anne* Atkins' is like a fingernail dragged across a blackboard. But a friend of mine is insulted when addressed with her husband's Christian name – and yet she didn't mind taking his surname. Other women object to using their husbands' surnames, while happily keeping their fathers'.

And the proposed solution to all this – 'Ms' – is of course quite horrid, very American, and sounds like a bee with a cold.

So if you really want to know, an unmarried girl is the only one you can really get right: 'Miss Sally Single'.

If she marries and keeps her maiden name for business, she stays the same. If she uses her married name, write to her at work as 'Miss (or Ms) Sally Spliced-Now', but at home, 'Mrs Simon Spliced-Now'. If in doubt, ask her what she prefers.

The only proper answer would have been for us to revert to the seventeenth century and call all women Mistress, with the written abbreviation Ms, just as all men are Mister, written Mr.

And of course etiquette, used properly, makes the wheels of social intercourse run much more smoothly.

DEAR ANNE – Please could you give me guidance on shaking hands? My friends think it is really weird, but my parents' friends do it all the time. So what do I do if I am introduced to somebody who appears to be somewhere in between? Jenny Brown (aged 15), Chichester

The correct behaviour is to wait and see whether the more senior person offers a hand. This solves everything. With your peer group, you needn't attempt it; with your elders, you need only do it if they do. (And with Eskimos, I think you rub noses.)

DEAR ANNE – After many years of coming to stay at our house, a guest has decided to bring her own marmalade because she says she doesn't like ours. A friend advises that when we visit her, we should make a show of taking Diocalm before each meal, whereas I am in favour of spraying her living room with air freshener. Have you a better suggestion? The trouble is we like the husband.
D.B., Kidlington

Give her a book of etiquette as a bread-and-butter present.

DEAR ANNE – Recently, I have received two messages on my answering machine, rather than letters, as thanks for dinner parties. Should I amend my views on etiquette, or delete these friends from my Filofax?
Helene Hammond, Kent

I'm tempted to say amend your Filofax, but let's be realistic. A generation or two ago, polite thank-you letters were written by women who were not trying to juggle jobs, children, board-meetings, plumbers, homes and childminders.

In theory, responses to formal invitations, overnight stays and presents should always be written. Strictly speaking, so should thank yous for dinners or weddings: after all, the hostess has gone to great trouble. Nevertheless, I'm usually thrilled if a busy friend rings me up and gushes over the telephone instead. It's certainly better than nothing – and a good chance to gossip about the party.

Bear in mind that others may have been brought up with different expectations: with the exception of my mother-in-law, my husband's family don't write letters or reply to invitations, ever; they just turn up – and why not? They're always fun to have around, and they themselves cook flexibly so it's not an issue.

You should always be far stricter on yourself than on others. If your friends forget to write, forgive them: just don't follow their example. And we should have a general moratorium for women with pre-school children, especially those with no domestic help. Juggling nappies with broken nights, broken vacuum cleaners, husbands, homes, etc, is enough to make anyone forget how to read and write.

DEAR ANNE – I was appalled to read two weeks ago that you excused guests who failed to write thank-you letters for dinner parties. It is absolute rubbish to say that a mother can be too busy with nappy-changing to have time to write – she had time to go out. Disgraceful. You are setting a very bad example.

To Helene Hammond of Kent who wrote in: delete those 'friends' from your Filofax. To you, Agony Atkins: good grief woman, your husband's family could do with an etiquette book.
Diana Francis-Jones, Wiltshire

Yessir. Sorree. I shall write Mrs Francis-Jones a formal letter of apology – as soon as I've got a spare moment.

DEAR ANNE – A few days ago, I picked up the phone to thank a friend for dinner – a practice which has been socially acceptable in my neck of the woods for years, and was greeted by her answerphone. I was about to hang up, when I remembered your response on the etiquette of this very subject. So I thanked her machine profusely and ended by telling it that this method was now perfectly acceptable – thanks to you.

With a smug look on my face, I then hunted for your column to fax to her. Imagine my horror when I re-read it and realized that you had merely said that telephone thank yous – not messages on answerphones – are better than nothing in this frantic world of ours. Please put me out of my misery – will I be struck from her Filofax?
Diane Rodger, Kent

Probably. Especially if she's a friend of Mrs Francis-Jones's. I suggest you write and apologize, too. And blame it all on me.

5. An Appalling Lack of Manners

It came as something of a surprise to me to discover readers who considered etiquette more important than the people it is there to serve – in particular, than the most vulnerable members of society, whom etiquette should surely protect more than any others: children.

DEAR ANNE – We have just been invited to the wedding of a good friend, which involves a whole day out in the country. The problem is that we have three children, aged five, ten and thirteen, and the invitation specifies: no children. I don't know what to do. If we don't go to the wedding, our friend will be extremely hurt. If we do, we would have to try to find friends prepared to look after the children – and we would feel terrible about not seeing them all day. My husband and I are with them little enough as it is, as we both work hard during the week. I have told our friend that we are having problems finding childcare, but she has not suggested that we take our brood along.
Mrs G.R., Manchester

It sounds as though you would prefer to be with your children. So would I. Decline the invitation on the grounds that because you work so hard, your weekend is sacrosanct to them. Your friend may be hurt, but she will survive without you. Your children will not. By excluding half of your family, your friend has already made her choice: your children were not given a choice at all. It is acceptable to make them a priority – and if it weren't, so what? You would rather have your children's good opinion of you than your friend's. All our friends know that we don't go anywhere on a Saturday without our brood: they have all six of us, or none. Sooner or later, let's hope, the message will get through and the English will abandon the extraordinary – and unnatural – custom of trying to enjoy themselves without their young. What on earth is the point of celebrating a wedding without living reminders of the most important and joyful result of the occasion?

My answer provoked an angry postbag in return.

DEAR ANNE – Your answer to the mother who was offended because her children were not invited to her friend's wedding was incredibly selfish. Has it not occurred to you – or her – that the reason children are not included is very often expense? If one couple brings their children, then it's unfair on everybody else if they cannot bring their offspring – and you could easily end up with more youngsters than adults at the reception. What happens to the offended mother's children when they are invited out by friends to birthday treats and the like? Do mummy and daddy tag along, too, or are the children not allowed to accept?
L.B., Guildford

DEAR ANNE – As usual, we enjoyed your column last week. But we feel we must take you up on one point. Maybe children are unwelcome at weddings because some British parents are unable to teach them how to behave in public …
G.P., Woking

DEAR ANNE – I really think you should apologize to the bride and her family immediately.
S.L., Lancashire

Rarely has this column provoked such outrage, but I am afraid that I am going to annoy you all further.

I explained that we, as a family, always spend Saturday evening together: if our friends can't accommodate our children in an invitation, they don't get us either – on that one evening of the week. L.B. has asked whether that means the children are expected to turn down invitations too, if mummy and daddy are not invited. No, they are not: if our children are invited out, they are free to accept. My husband and I choose not to be. We need to be available for them; they don't need to be there for us.

In addition, while friends are important, children are far more so, because they are dependent on us. This is not selfish, but responsible. As friends, we may influence others' opinions; as workers, we fulfil a role in society; but as parents, we shape our children's entire lives.

It is sadly true that children sometimes behave inappropriately, though adults often behave worse: one seldom sees grown-ups being told to rush their food, or being ignored in conversation. It is also interesting that in places such as Ireland, Italy or Africa, where children are liked and expected to mingle with adults, children tend to behave much better.

Lastly, I think that a wedding with more children than adults would be an utterly delightful prospect – especially if sausages, soft drinks and even perhaps a conjurer (cheaper than champagne) are available. At my own wedding, when the minister asked for any just causes, my husband's little cousin cried, 'Shoe' (having momentarily mislaid her own by bowling it down the aisle). The building was King's Chapel, Cambridge, designed to magnify a child's voice for seven seconds, but happily her objection was not considered a sufficient impediment…

A society that has grown so rich that it can no longer afford its children must also be so selfish that it deserves to expire. Given the declining birth rate, it probably soon will.

But this backlash in turn prompted another backlash.

DEAR ANNE – Oh, how I agree with your rebuke of the selfish 'adult only' wedding set.
S.G., Bath

Thank you for all the advice and letters about children and weddings. My own theories were put to the test last Saturday, when our church organist celebrated her wedding. The couple's house is tiny, so we hosted the reception in our vicarage garden.

What was interesting was the startling difference between the Western European and Asian cultures. The bride is Korean, the groom German, most of our congregation British, so the guests a mixture of all three.

A number of the European parents politely rang me beforehand, to ask whether their children could come – to which the answer was, of course, yes. Most intriguingly, though Koreans exemplify excessively good manners, not one of them asked me this, presumably because it would never occur to any of them in a month of Sundays that any parents could be mad enough to leave their children behind, if there is a wedding in the offing.

And I have to admit that, though some of the children behaved beautifully, others did not. My favourite item of furniture was broken, our children's bedrooms were trashed, and my lovely old birdbath is in pieces after a toddler pushed it over. It's a miracle it didn't kill one of them. You may say it serves me right.

But without exception, the Korean children – who accompany their parents everywhere, always – behaved like little angels.

We get the children we deserve.

Having publicised how we try to spend our Saturdays, I felt I had to reply to this, which arrived via the *Telegraph*.

DEAR ANNE – Some time ago, you challenged a critic to feed you at the Ritz. If he has not taken you up on this yet, we would love to give you and your husband dinner sometime. How about Saturday?
C.T., London SW6

Only if you can also cope with four – not always well behaved – children. And week nights are no good either, because we have to get them up for school the next day. Any Friday would be stunning.

(We did indeed go on a Friday.)

But the last word, of gentle compromise, should go to Mrs Attenborough, from whom I recently received this.

I would be very happy for my contribution to be included in your book, but it never appeared in your column, probably because you received a number of letters on the subject. I felt rather sorry for the questioner, because you came down very definitely on the side of inviting whole families. As the mother of a bride who had been unable to do this because of numbers and expense, I wrote to tell you about the informal reception in our home which took place sometime after the wedding, and to which we invited families with children.
(Mrs) Ruth Attenborough, Chelmsford

Nonetheless, the patter of little feet continued to run through the question of weddings.

DEAR ANNE – I am planning my wedding, and my sister would love her daughter (who is just two) to be my bridesmaid. She is very cute, but a bit of a liability, and I'm not sure if she would really be acceptable. Would the vicar object, for instance?
A.H., Berkshire

I should jolly well hope not. You should, of course, respect his authority regarding the service, but even the most dictatorial old cleric wouldn't dream of vetoing the bride's choice of attendants.

She sounds gorgeous. I don't think you should worry at all.

But if you are still concerned and really don't want to risk any unscripted just causes, you could provide a crèche and ask her to accompany you only at the beginning and the end of the service.

And the debate about invitations was not over yet, either.

DEAR ANNE – Next weekend, friends of ours are having their first baby christened. They have invited us to the ceremony and lunch.

Originally, I asked if our teenage children could come. They are both weekly boarders, so Sundays are precious family times. The hostess said there wasn't really room in their small house, but added that she was confident we would enjoy ourselves more without our children – a comment I found quite hurtful.

I have just discovered that two other families are attending with their young children – presumably because they are too small to be left behind. There is nothing I want less, now, than to go without my children. Would it be churlish to stay away? Am I getting the situation out of proportion?
Name and address supplied

Yes and no. I understand your reaction, but you must try to make allowances for your hostess. She has shown an appalling lack of manners and imagination, but she did not deliberately set out to make you or your children feel rejected. She isn't making a statement about them personally, but about teenagers in general – a view one hopes she'll change in 13 years' time.

Your mistake was to accept the invitation at all. Now you have done so, you had better go. You can always take your children to the church service, then you and your husband can briefly raise a glass of champagne to the baby over lunch and quietly slip out before pudding.

And in future, keep your weekends sacrosanct. If you are invited out without your children, simply say no – and explain why.

DEAR ANNE – It is a bit rich to accuse a hostess of having an 'appalling lack of manners' for not inviting your correspondent's children to her child's christening (19 November).

As any etiquette expert will tell you, a host or hostess may extend invitations to whomever he or she wishes. A faux pas is committed only when an invitation is extended to one half of a married couple but not the other; children are not automatically included in their parents' invitations.
Vicky Larmour, Cambridge

You are absolutely right, strictly speaking. However, I did not accuse the hostess of a technical breach of etiquette, but of a lack of real manners. Etiquette dictates the correct code of behaviour for a given situation and is useful when we are not sure how to behave. But manners are harder to legislate for and much more important: they dictate kindness and unselfishness, and how to make others feel appreciated.

The hostess could easily have explained why other, younger children were invited. She almost certainly could have squeezed a couple of teenagers in. And there was no need for her to justify her restriction by suggesting the mother would be happier without her children – which was downright rude. She is entitled to invite whom she wishes. But what is the point if her guests are miserable?

Children continued to challenge the rules of etiquette:

DEAR ANNE – My husband and I are having our first child in a few weeks and, naturally, I am planning to feed the baby myself.

I had thought that nowadays it was acceptable to breast-feed almost anywhere, but my sister insists it is the height of bad manners to do so in public. In fact, we had quite a heated debated about it. She claims *Debrett's* is on her side. I dread the thought of retreating into solitary confinement whenever my baby is hungry. Please could you help resolve this dispute?
J.T., Bridgnorth

Debrett's is right 99 per cent of the time – and 100 per cent wrong on this. Most people are charmed: they are aware that modern mothers are staggeringly busy, and glad that the baby is getting a healthy meal. Normal manners apply, of course. Be aware of others' sensitivities, particularly the older generation. If in doubt, put their feelings before your own convenience. At someone else's dinner party, ask your hostess first. And so on.

Above all, be discreet. Wear a loose top and feed the baby under it, and many people won't even notice what you are doing.

DEAR ANNE – I was dismayed to read in your column (5 November) that the older generation might be sensitive to breast-feeding in public. We were brought up seeing our mothers and sisters doing it. It's the young that are priggish.

Breast-feeding is safe, nutritious, convenient and cheap. It doesn't matter where you do it.
Mr R.H. Jarrett, Kent

When I said we should be sensitive to the older generation, I didn't mean that senior citizens are more prudish – simply more important. If older people do object to something, their feelings should be taken into account.

However, while I believe that we should teach children manners by extending good manners to them – something we seem to find remarkably difficult – I agree that we sometimes have to use more proactive measures. (I didn't, incidentally, know who or what Buzz Lightyear was, but my editor explained that it was the thing for Christmas that year … with remarkably aggressive, nasty corners.)

DEAR ANNE – My four-year-old throws toys at his little sister. Buzz Lightyear has sharp edges, so it makes her cry. How can I persuade him to stop doing this?
P. Hodges, Exeter

Tell him you'll smack him if he does it again.

DEAR ANNE – As you suggested, I threatened my son with a smack if he kept on throwing Buzz Lightyear at his little sister. He did it anyway. What now?
P. Hodges, Exeter

Smack him.

DEAR ANNE – I did as you said, and smacked my four-year-old for bullying his sister. The trouble is, he smacked me back.
P. Hodges, Exeter

That's why God made you bigger.

6. Hand Him the Spoon

After such advice, the following was as inevitable as Pavlov's dogs slobbering at dinnertime.

DEAR ANNE – As a mother of three and a former primary school head, I was very concerned about you advising a parent to smack her four-year-old. Yes, I have smacked my own children occasionally, and even my pupils when it was allowed. But over the years, I have realized that violence breeds violence. During my teaching time, I saw horrific things being done to children by both parents and teachers. One child was thrown against a wall and others were publicly humiliated or regularly made to stand in corners. In my last school, which was the happiest I worked in, I encouraged the children to help each other and to be tolerant. We had high expectations and a system of praise, incentives and clear punishments. There really are more effective chastisements than smacking.
S.B., Leeds

A smack is not violence – and does not breed violence. This mantra, 'violence breeds violence', is constantly being reiterated by anti-smacking pressure groups (though of course they always insist on calling it 'hitting', presumably because they can't tell the difference); but no evidence has ever been produced – and I'm sure never will be – that suggests that children who have been given tactile punishments are any more aggressive than those who are disciplined in other ways.

Sadly, because we're all 'fallen' human beings, we all require restraints, particularly in our formative years. Children over the age of about six months need (and long) to know where the boundaries are. Indeed, if the limits are unclear, youngsters will push until they find them. So parents' rules should be: clear (defined and explained); loving (in the child's interests); and enforced (carrying consequences if ignored). This means that occasionally we need unpleasant, but harmless, deterrents. It doesn't much matter what they are, provided you ensure they are administered kindly and intelligently.

If you don't like smacking, don't use it. I certainly wouldn't advise it in schools (apart from anything else, as you rightly point out, it is now illegal); and of course all teachers should be encouraging their pupils to help each other and be tolerant. But the occasional slap from a self-controlled, loving parent will no more turn a child into a mugger than confiscating his toys will turn him into a kleptomaniac. A fair and calmly given slap is as similar to hurling a child against a wall as an affectionate kiss is like sexual abuse. A reasonable punishment is not the same as a random act of vandalism, and any normal, properly brought-up child knows this. Publicly humiliating a child, by contrast, is a dreadful violation of his dignity, and almost always counterproductive. The same is true of shouting.

For children between the ages of about two and six, smacking is effective, readily understood and over quicker than any other punishment. When I gave my children the choice, they usually opted for a smack rather than a long drawn-out alternative. But we should never, ever smack a child to relieve our own feelings.

If you are cross, hand over to your spouse, stomp around the garden, put your head in a bucket of cold water, or scream – but not at the child. Raised voices damage children far more than a calmly dispensed slap.

DEAR ANNE – The other day my wife rang me at work, distraught at having smacked one of our four sons (who are aged two to eight). She was in tears, suggesting I ought to report her to the social services, and claiming that she was not fit to look after our children alone.

I calmed her down, and reassured her that she was a wonderful mother. The boys weren't at all upset. The older ones said the five-year-old had well and truly asked for it – though I suspect they were all being impossible.

Did she do wrong, and can you suggest any guidelines in case she reaches the end of her tether again?
M.H., Norwich

Of course she didn't do wrong. Discipline involves teaching, example, reward and punishment. There is not a child living who doesn't need disincentives. With young children, you can withhold treats or send them to their rooms; but a smack is quicker, often more effective, and – most important of all – enables you to put the misdemeanour in the past immediately. The only thing wrong with smacking is that it is out of fashion.

I suspect what upset your wife was that she momentarily lost control. Ideally, we should never discipline our children in anger. Punishments should always be for the benefit of the child, never because the adult has lost his temper. Nevertheless, there probably isn't a parent in the world who hasn't occasionally done so. As long as it doesn't happen too often, and the lack of control isn't dangerous, and we apologize afterwards, and the rest of the time give our children the loving and security and self-worth they need, they will recover from an occasional loss of temper as surely as they recover from a grazed knee when they fall over.

You did the most important and constructive thing you could by telling your wife what a terrific mother she is. I suggest you buy her a huge bunch of flowers, and say it again. The best thing you can do for your children is let them know how much you love their mother.

If you want to do more, why not draw up a list of rules and punishments with her. Tell the boys what they are. Then she (and they) will know she is not reacting in the heat of the moment. If in doubt, she can count to ten and breathe deeply. Tell her to ring you at work whenever she wants. Nothing on your desk is more important than your wife and sons.

And never, *ever* involve social services in your family affairs. Wonderful and necessary though they often are, they can do infinitely more harm to a happy family than a hundred smacks.

I ought perhaps to add that since this was written, the law in England and Wales has changed slightly. Contrary to now confused and quite unnecessarily guilty public opinion, it is still legal for a parent to smack a child. It is illegal to leave a mark of more than transitory duration.

Nowadays, of course, a parent can find himself guilty of apparent child abuse before he's even woken up in the morning. Tragically, this can blunt our sensitivities to the genuine and very terrible article.

DEAR ANNE – A long time ago, I was sexually abused by some men, and since then I have felt disgusted with myself for allowing it to happen. Now, I feel like killing myself; I have tried to before, but I was stopped. Please help.
P.L., aged 12, London

You must ask for help from your family and friends. Tell an adult immediately: preferably your parents; otherwise a sympathetic teacher, or perhaps a friend or relative considerably older than you. You can also ring Childline on 0800 1111 (persevere until you get through) but don't make this a substitute for telling someone face to face.

You must also see your GP, and describe the emotions you are experiencing. It is best if you can go with your mother or father; but if for some reason you can't do this, you can make an appointment by yourself. If you don't know how to contact your GP, ask for help from someone at school, such as the nurse or your class teacher. Your doctor will want to make sure you are safe and may want you to see a child psychologist. It is not your fault you were abused, and you must keep telling yourself this. You have not done wrong.

To kill yourself, however, would be very wrong indeed. Those men who abused you did not value you properly; don't add to what they did by not valuing yourself. There are others in your life who treasure you very much and who would be devastated to lose you: your family, your schoolfriends, your teachers. Your life is a precious gift, and you must never throw it away.

Sadly, suicidal feelings are more common among the young than ever before.

DEAR ANNE – Our teenage daughter has an unstable school-friend, who is constantly in trouble. A few months ago, the girl slit her wrists – though she was taken to hospital before she had done too much damage.

Our daughter now wants to leave school (without doing A-levels) and is threatening to do the same if we don't yield. One should always take suicide threats seriously, but my instinct is that my daughter doesn't really intend to carry hers out.

What should we do?
Name and address supplied

You are right: never ignore a child who mentions taking his or her own life. It always indicates a need – the skill is in working out what the need is. Almost certainly, your instinct that she doesn't intend to carry it out is also correct, but in a sense this doesn't make any difference to the course of action you should take.

Start by sitting her down and explaining that suicide is wrong, so must never be either contemplated, or threatened as a means to manipulate people. I should also insist that she visits your GP, on the grounds that suicidal thoughts indicate depression, which should be treated. Possibly she should be referred to a child psychologist.

You must also make it clear that you put her welfare above anything else. She may be genuinely distressed at the thought of more studying, and perhaps needs to change school. She could certainly do with more wholesome friends; you don't want to encourage her to abandon the unhappy ones, but she may not be mature enough to cope with their problems.

Above all, give her the time and attention she wants. She has sent out a cry for help. You shouldn't necessarily give in to her demands, but you must try to meet her needs.

DEAR ANNE – When my mother died nine years ago, my daughter took it badly. Soon afterwards, she became involved with drugs and took an overdose. I still don't think that she understands the anguish that she put us through; I will never forget the sight of my husband in tears that day.

Then, just as we thought the situation had improved a little, she announced that she was a lesbian.

She is now at university and is having an affair with a girl she knew at school. I know I should accept that she's homosexual and feel glad that she is feeling happier, but I can't bear the thought that she might always be a lesbian.

If you think you are gay in your teens, does that mean you will be that way for the rest of your life?
Name and address supplied

Plenty of people have felt homosexual desires in their teens before going on to experience only heterosexual desires in later life. But this is less likely to happen after a period of homosexual practice and identity.

What matters is that your daughter has suffered great pain. Try to give her unconditional love, which means accepting her as she is. She may change her orientation or she may not, but she is unlikely to do so as a result of pressure from you – whether spoken or unspoken.

The fact that she didn't realize how much her suicide attempt would hurt you is highly significant: her greatest need is to know how much she matters to you. She longs to know that you love her, and that means everything about her – even her homosexuality. (This does not necessarily mean you approve of what she *does*: but you do have to try to accept who she *is*.)

I realize what a challenge this is. When we were first told that one of our children had a disability I went through a period of bereavement, which I believe is quite common: I had to say goodbye to the child I'd thought I had, in order to love the one I really had. As it happens, I soon realized how much more interesting and unusual he is the way God made him, and that his supposed "disability" is in fact a unique and wonderful difference. After that I wouldn't have changed him for the world (though I've often wished I could change society, and its attitude towards him).

Whether or not your daughter might one day change, you've got to learn to love the person she is now. You got her back from the brink of death. Remember what nearly happened, and you will surely be grateful for what happened instead.

Usually, I loved getting letters from children. But obviously not either of these:

DEAR ANNE – I am a 13-year-old boy. At the end of the holidays, I became very depressed and ran away to avoid going back to school. I had clothes and various other items with me, including a penknife. After six hours, the police tracked me down. When I saw their car, I tried to slit my wrists, but the police caught up with me so I slipped the knife into my pocket. Then they escorted me home.

As soon as I got back, I locked myself in the bathroom and took about 25 tablets of something in the hope that I would die quickly and painlessly. I didn't, obviously.

Nobody else knows of these two attempts, and now I am OK and have put it all in the past. But, occasionally, I feel in the mood to try again, with more success than before. I know it's wrong and selfish, but I am worried that I may do something stupid without thinking about it, and then it will be too late. Please tell me what I should do.
Name and address withheld

I cannot emphasize this enough: *get help*. The obvious people to talk to are your parents: they love you, and are more committed than anyone else to helping you. As well as this, you should ask them to take you to see an experienced, professional adult so you can explain what you have been going through, starting with your GP. If, for any reason, you can't tell your parents or they don't give you all the help you need, you can go to your GP yourself; you could also talk to your school nurse, headteacher or another member of staff. The point is that you must tell someone, and preferably several people in case the first person you confide in doesn't know what to do.

Your GP ought to refer you to a child psychologist, who can help you discover what is making you feel like this and, if you have other problems, will help you to talk about them. Sometimes, depression can be caused by a simple chemical imbalance, for which you may need prescribed medication.

Do ask for help immediately. And please send me your name and address, so that I can contact you to make sure that you are all right.

He never did, alas. I can only hope and pray that he read the column, and got some help from somewhere. And that he is still around and perhaps, one day, might read this … and even let me know how he's getting on.

My answer to this dreadfully sad question was always the same.

DEAR ANNE – Some time ago, I went to see Backstreet Boys at Wembley – I am a huge fan. Afterwards, I got really depressed and cried myself to sleep several nights in a row. Finally, it all got too much for me and I went into the bathroom and tried to slash my wrist. Luckily, I did not cut myself badly and managed to stop the bleeding, but I'm still really depressed.

I can't talk to my mother about this as she will go mad, and I'm also too scared to talk to my friends in case they tell her. Please help.
S.P. (12), London W10

You must talk to someone. I would be very surprised if your mother were cross with you – but she might be upset because she loves you so much. Adults sometimes seem angry when in fact they are really distressed or frightened. So I urge you to confide in her, because she and your father are best placed to help you.

You could also talk to another adult, preferably one who knows you well, such as your doctor, vicar or teacher. Any of these will probably want to let your parents know how you feel, but they should ask your permission first.

By all means talk to your friends as well, but don't make that a substitute for getting adult help.

Never ever attempt suicide. As a solution, it's a non-starter; as a cry for help, it is very dangerous and can go horribly wrong.

I'm not sure why seeing the Backstreet Boys made you so upset, but may I tentatively suggest you follow another group that might make you more cheerful? Life is too short for hobbies that make us cry ourselves to sleep.

DEAR ANNE – How can an inexperienced child differentiate between two painful experiences – say, sexual abuse and vaccination, or other medical procedures – the one traumatic for life, and the other only temporarily so? How can a small child know that abuse is not a normal pattern of life? Many fathers and daughters have legitimate secrets together. This is an academic question.
R. Bowers, Gloucestershire

The awesome answer is that a child can't. If you have only a few years' experience of the world, you have no way of knowing that schoolfriends are not supposed to be unkind to you, that teachers shouldn't shout at you, or men abuse you sexually. You can know only that it hurts – and yet, as you point out, some forms of pain are for our own good. This gives adults an almost unbearable responsibility for children. If an adult is determined to abuse a child, he or she will probably succeed, at least for a while. So we must constantly be vigilant about the welfare of children. Parents should encourage their children to discuss anything

– even be free to say: 'I hate you Mummy.' Nothing our children say to us should ever be too shocking, or too trivial, or too wicked for them to share with us.

Sadly though, they still may not. Children are sometimes too unhappy or worried to talk freely. So it's up to us: all grown-ups should be alert to signs that a child is depressed, or under-achieving, or ill.

As this correspondent pointed out, a child cannot know what constitutes abuse. (But then, more and more adults don't necessarily seem able to work it out either ...)

DEAR ANNE – I have had a pen pal in Arkansas, America, for nearly two years, and she has become a close friend. But I am worried that she is being abused. She was recently punished at school by being 'paddled' – spanked on her bottom. She didn't seem particularly upset, and said she chose this punishment rather than be suspended. Is there any serious advice I could pass on to help her? Or do you think this isn't as bad as I think? Helen A., aged 12, Lincs

I think it is brilliant of you to be so responsible and concerned about her. However, I don't think you have any cause for concern. Being punished is very different from being abused. A fair smack, given in a controlled manner, is a perfectly reasonable punishment for a misdemeanour, and plenty of sensible people would choose this in preference to more drawn-out punishments.

Your friend made the obvious choice – one that is, of course, no longer available to British school-children.

So, I shouldn't worry too much. However, I suggest that you tell her you were surprised because physical punishment isn't allowed in British schools. Ask how she felt, how hard she was hit and how quickly she got over it. You could also tell her about Childline, and ask whether they have anything similar in Arkansas. If you are still worried, please write to me again.

When children wrote to me with serious problems, I always felt that the best I could do was refer them to the adults who were there to help them. Although this was the only proper course of action open to me, it was inevitably risky, because adults are only fallible human beings.

DEAR ANNE – Please help me. I am 12, and I keep wetting my knickers. Last week, it happened in school. I am too embarrassed to talk to my father's girlfriend, but I have told my teacher, who says I'll grow out of it.
J., West Midlands

This problem is far more common than you might think. I'm sorry your teacher wasn't more help; why not go to your school nurse or doctor, or see your GP – you can ask for a woman GP, which might be easier for you.

I wonder if you should also pluck up your courage to talk to your father's girlfriend, too? She may be far more sympathetic than you expect. It would be a good idea to take her into your confidence, if you can, since you also ought to have someone you feel able to talk to about your periods, if you have any queries.

DEAR ANNE – Please tell the 12-year-old who wrote to you because she was worried about bedwetting to contact the Association for Continence Advice 0141 434 1500 (info@aca.uk).
Joan McIntosh, Essex

Thank you for this information. This will surely be an excellent place to start, although it is still very important that she receives medical help. Her GP and school nurse should be invaluable allies.

Sometimes I was sent problems that shouldn't have been problems at all:

DEAR ANNE – I have a best friend called Julie. Everything she does makes me happy: her smile, her noise, her actions, even her anger. When we have arguments and make up afterwards, we just get closer. I feel as if our friendship can never be broken. Now I've just started in year eight, and I'm not in the same class as Julie any more. I sometimes cry myself to sleep. I share my thoughts with my dog, but it doesn't help. How can I sustain our friendship?
Sandra, aged 12, London W3

You are very lucky to have Julie. Friendship is precious and you should treasure it. Don't worry that you aren't together all the time. You still have break, lunch, and weekends, and it may be an advantage being in different forms. You might find you can concentrate better and work harder without the distraction of your best friend being there. Try to make other friends, too, but do maintain your friendship with Julie: maybe your parents would let you do your homework together sometimes after school, or you could go to the cinema on Saturdays. It's possible for your friendship to last for years. I still love my best friend from school very much. Our lives and outlook have changed considerably and sometimes we don't see each other for a year or more. But when we meet, we pick up as if we'd never left off.

DEAR ANNE – I am worried about one of my hobbies. I find computer programming very interesting, and a teacher from my last school gave me an old BBC computer, on which I am inventing various games and programmes.

But nobody else in my family understands computers. My mother gets cross if I'm late for meals because I'm working at my PC and I think they all consider me a 'computer nerd'. This makes me very upset.
A.A. (12), London

It can be very lonely being born with a talent that nobody in your family shares: your family has to try to understand your concerns, and you must do the same with theirs.

Start by making sure that you are never late for a meal. Instead, make a point of arriving early and offering to help. If you find this difficult because you become absorbed in your computing, set an alarm to go off 15 or 30 minutes before each meal.

Make sure you have other interests, too. Computing is both solitary and sedentary, so in the holidays spend time with other people and take plenty of exercise.

Lastly, have fun: make a game for each member of your family, and teach them how to play them. Share what you love with the people you love and, in time, they will learn to enjoy your hobby, too.

OK, I confess. This last letter was from my son. He's still a computer genius, and he's still late for every single meal. And he has never succeeded in getting me to learn anything on a computer, at all. I can't even find the elastic band at the back to wind it up. My mother says he must suffer like a musician living amongst the deaf.

He has very kindly and supportively provided the following update for me.

Your advice was completely useless. How can I set an alarm to go off half an hour before a meal in this house, when dinner could be served any time between seven and eleven, and even the person cooking it doesn't know when it's going to be until five minutes after we're all late for it? Unless that person is me. Which is why I try to do most of the cooking. And as for trying to teach you how to play a computer game ... [resigned sigh and shake of head]
J. Alexander D. Atkins

But I did not, positively not, write this next letter to myself.

DEAR ANNE – Every time I spoon food into our baby's mouth, my own mouth opens and closes like a goldfish. It really annoys my husband. How can I stop?
Hassled mum

Hand him the spoon.

"It's harder than you think, isn't it?"

7. Has the Weekend Been and Gone?

As I say, I did not write that last letter to myself. All the letters in my column were absolutely, one hundred per cent bona fide. Real people with real problems.

Funnily enough, however, I had a friend who used to give me very interesting advice. If anything went wrong in my own life or I had a difficult decision to make, he kindly said I was so good at helping others that I should simply imagine I was a stranger applying to myself for help.

Well, one dreadful Monday morning, I went to my desk and found a horror that Alexander had obviously rigged up to frighten me with before returning to school the night before. It was a very nasty, underhand, clever device with the transparently evil intention of trying to bully me into both working at my next book and looking after my computer, at the same time.

It was after nine in the morning, he would be in Maths or Greek already, and there was nowhere else I could turn for help. There was, in fact, absolutely nothing I could do.

Except write to myself.

DEAR ANNE – I am a writer. My 13-year-old is always nagging me about 'screen saving', and telling me to do tedious things to protect my monitor that are, frankly, too boring to remember.

Today, I turned on my computer to do a morning's work in the normal way – looking out of the window, sharpening pencils, making coffee; the innocent rough and tumble of the writer's harmless existence – to find that, if ever I stopped typing for more than twenty seconds, I was terrorized by woolly mammoths in red hats, paragliding across my screen and blowing raspberries, bouncing up and down on pogo sticks with appropriate sound effects, driving aeroplanes and crashing penny-farthing bicycles into the peace and quiet of my study. I write this even now in a state of nervous terror, knowing they will come at me again if I even so much as pause for a moment's thought.

My computer-literate son is back at boarding school. I've already had to ask the school secretary to pull him out of lessons once before when I couldn't remember how to turn my computer on. I am too embarrassed to do it again. Can you help?
A.A., London, SW

There is nothing for it, I'm afraid. You will have to keep typing as if your life depended on it.

I was not the only one to suffer at my desk.

DEAR ANNE – It's exam time and I'm getting really stressed – my hair is falling out, I'm suffering terrible mood swings and I can't sleep at night for worry that my grades won't be good enough to get me into university. I try going for walks to help clear my mind, but this gets me even more stressed as I feel that I am wasting valuable time. Can you suggest any quick relaxation techniques that won't make me feel guilty for taking time out? F.D., Buckinghamshire

Jiminy Cricket, give yourself a break! I used to reckon that the more important the exam, the more time off I needed before it. So, for my degree, I finished revising a week before the first paper and then went home to my parents' to take it easy. I also believe in enjoying exams as much as possible: on the morning of my husband's (then fiancé's) first Finals paper, I used up half a term's grant giving him a breakfast of champagne, smoked salmon, strawberries, and a few ounces of real caviar – and a red rose for his button hole, of course – and he still maintains he was the most relaxed person in the exam hall.

I could give you relaxation exercises – lie on your back, slow your breathing, imagine your limbs filling up with liquid lead or everyone else in the exam room keeling over and expiring in a sea of green vomit, and all that hypno-suggestive stuff – but I suspect what you really need is a funda-mental change of attitude. First, look to your health. Your GP would probably give you a limited supply of mild sleeping pills to break your insomnia and might suggest a better diet, or even nutritional supplements, to help with your hair loss.

Then, draw up a timetable. Plan your revision. Aim to spend as much time relaxing as working. Have sensible, unrushed meals. Spend the evening before each exam as far away from books as possible – a long walk is a good idea, as is playing the piano or watching a comedy on television. Have an early night. Be firm and disciplined and tell yourself that this approach is almost certainly improving your grades. After each exam, give yourself a treat – enjoy a cream tea with a friend or a picnic by the river.

And bear in mind that most people in the world survive perfectly well without a university degree.

During the summer term of my first year at university, I was going back to my rooms one morning during the exam season, when I saw police cordons around the University Church and a tarpaulin covering a bundle on the ground. How is it possible, I asked myself, for exams to be more important than life? How can a degreeless existence possibly be worse than no existence at all? How can anyone think it impossible to do without something that most of the world has never heard of?

These are, of course, questions without answers, but they are questions that are worth remembering, nonetheless.

DEAR ANNE – Our daughter is 16 and at boarding school, preparing for her GCSEs. Last week, she nearly took her own life.

Obviously, we are feeling rather shaken, but the school thinks we should not disrupt her routine, as she may never have the courage to go through with her GCSEs another time if she pulls out now. My instinct was to bring her home, but perhaps I'm just being selfish.

People at the school are being very kind, but I'm not sure if they appreciate the seriousness of the situation, or whether I'm exaggerating. Please help, as we just don't know what to do.
Name and address withheld

For goodness' sake, if your instinct is to bring her home then *bring her home*. What do her GCSEs matter, as long as she is alive? I dare say the teachers are wise and experienced, and it's possible that your daughter would be better to keep going. But suppose she isn't? The stakes are simply too high. If you are still wavering, just imagine the future if the teachers happen to be wrong.

There is no doubt in my mind as to the wisest course of action. Collect your daughter immediately and bring her home. Pamper her and look after her, as your instinct tells you to. Take her to your GP for proper medical advice on her mood and vulnerability. Ask her what she wants.

She doesn't necessarily have to abandon her exams. There is still time before they are due to begin, and you have a number of options. She could sit them near home. Or she could go back to school when the exams start, and you could accompany her to give her ongoing support. She could do just some of them. Or she could give them all a go on the understanding that she can resit them if she wishes. And if she doesn't do them this year, so what? Of course she will have the courage later, if she wants to.

Alternatively she could forget exams altogether and go without. Lots of people have fulfilled lives without them, but no one has a fulfilled life after a successful suicide.

Exams offer unparalleled opportunity for worry, anxiety and agony.

This next letter came after Gordon Brown had just made a spectacular ass of himself over Oxford University's admissions procedure. (One of the many excellent candidates who had been turned down that year because of pressure on places, Laura Spence, happened to come from a comprehensive in the North of England. So Mr Brown concluded – as one does – that this was not so much because there had been even better candidates who deserved the places even more, nor even because grades have been so inflated that top universities are bound to have to turn down lots of candidates with all A grades – especially for medicine which the government puts a quota on – but because Oxford Admissions Tutors have a funny thing about comprehensives in the North of England. Obviously.)

DEAR ANNE – My A-levels are about to begin, and they are going to seriously upset my social life: my mother is telling me I've got to go to bed early, refuse all invitations and stop going out drinking with friends. Please, help.
Molly Johnson, Leeds

No problem. Transfer to what is known as a 'sink school'. (I'm not sure what these are, but they're always in the papers so it shouldn't be hard to find one.) Go out every night and do no work at all. When you want to apply to a top university, simply send your details to Gordon Brown and the *Daily Mirror* and you should be fine. (PS: I note with approval that you are already splitting your infinitives. That's the spirit!)

DEAR ANNE – Our Latin exams are all scheduled to last for three hours. Unfortunately, the exam takes only an hour and a half to complete, check, recheck and check again. Our school won't let us leave early. How does one cope with the tedium?
Kate Henley (17), Oxford

Your school is being most unreasonable, if I may say so. One or two of our exams were so easy-peasy (even in those days) that we would turn up halfway through to give the examiner a sporting chance. I also remember having to leave a university entrance exam long before the end, as I had a prior commitment to attend a tea party.

Write a sonnet. A good one might fill ninety minutes and you would remember it easily afterwards, obviating the need to smuggle bits of paper out.

DEAR ANNE – I have just finished my GCSEs. How can I celebrate without breaking the law?
Annabel, North London

Help someone old, learn something new, try something borrowed, and dye your hair blue.

Exams, of course, are only a recent worry; there are other issues that have troubled teenagers since the dawn of time.

DEAR ANNE – I am a 15-year-old schoolboy who has never had a girlfriend. But now I have met a girl I really like and I suspect she feels the same way. Soon, there is the senior ball at school and I would really like to take her to it as my partner.

The problem is that she is not the most fashionable girl in the year, and is frankly thought of as being rather sad. I know I would lose a lot of face if I went out with her – my friends would never stop taking the mickey. But I really love her, so I feel torn.

I'm sorry if this sounds trivial but I don't know who else to ask.

H.S., London

It is not trivial at all. We all wrestle with such dilemmas, in one form or another, as soon as we become aware of the opinions of others.

You need to decide whether you want to please your friends or yourself. Choosing to please your friends will make you feel fashionable but miserable: if you doubt me, try reading Daphne du Maurier's *Rebecca*, which describes how the most desirable woman around made her husband the envy of the neighbourhood – and also wrecked his life.

It is true that pleasing yourself may make you feel slightly awkward to begin with; you may even lose the respect of your friends. But I'm sure that they will be secretly impressed if you ignore them and stick to your guns. And if they aren't, you will still feel independent, free and content.

When women are admired, they blossom. Look after your girlfriend well, and she will soon be coveted by others. If anyone suggests the slightest insult to her while she is out with you, have no hesitation in offering the offender a black eye.

And you will find, when you walk into the senior ball with your preferred girl on your arm, that you suddenly don't care very much what your friends think after all.

DEAR ANNE – I am the eldest child in my family. Every so often, my parents go out, leaving me in charge of my younger brothers and sisters (yesterday, they were at a parents' evening).

This is reasonable, because I babysit for other people's children and enjoy it – and also get paid. But looking after my own siblings is a disaster.

Last night, I tried to get my youngest brother to do his piano practice. He told me to leave him alone, and when I asked my sister to help me out, she refused. Then they were all rude about my cooking and wouldn't help me clear up. Finally, my other brother rang Childline because I wouldn't let him eat the last yoghurt, and he thought this might qualify as abuse.

I got very upset and felt I never wanted to look after them again.

It would be stupid for my parents to get a babysitter, because we aren't babies any more. Please tell me how to cope.
C.S.E.A., London (nearly 16)

In one sense, you and your siblings are equal: presumably when your parents are in charge, you all muck in and don't have a problem. But when you are left alone with them, you all have to readjust your relationships because you – as the eldest – are in a position of authority. That's why it's easier to deal with other people's children – they don't have to make this shift. Talk to your parents about these problems, and ask them to share out some of the responsibility. They should make it clear to your brother that if he doesn't do his practice, he will get into trouble – not you. And if you have done the cooking, someone else should do the washing-up.

Also, why not ask your parents to give you more pocket money than the younger ones to reflect

"Is that Childline? Do you do babysitting?"

your senior status? They shouldn't necessarily pay you to babysit – we all have to pull our weight in any household – but they might increase your allowance in gratitude for your helpfulness.

As I reread this, it struck me that those initials look familiar. Oh, of course: our eldest is also a C.S.E.A. What an extraordinary coincidence ...

Parents obviously often share the same worries as their teenagers. The following answer landed me in big trouble. Spot the idiocy.

DEAR ANNE – Ever since the summer holidays, our 15-year-old has been asking if she can have an allowance. Her friends at school seem to have this arrangement with their parents, and then spend their money on body-piercing, weird hairdos and frightful clothes.

Naturally, we are worried that our daughter will do the same. At present, we give her pocket money for little trifles, but pay for all her necessities as and when she needs them – which gives us some control. But she still keeps asking and I am not sure how long I can go on putting this off. What should we do?

B.S., Esher

I can't see why you want to put it off. Allowances are wonderfully liberating – particularly for the parents. Weird hair and hideous clothes won't do your daughter any harm at all, and you can specify that she is not to mutilate her body until she is of age.

The amount can be anything from £30 to £70 a month, depending on what you can afford and what she must pay for. Work this out carefully in advance: does it include toiletries, travel, summer camp, clothes, sheet music and books? If so, it should be on the generous side. Do you want to promise more if she keeps her room tidy, improves her homework, and helps with the housework? In which case, allow for an increase. Do you want to specify certain things she is not to spend it on?

The poor child will soon be an adult: so let her get used to a little independence. Provided you have brought her up sensibly so far, the more freedom you can give her now, the better.

This letter was fairly early on in the history of the column, and what happened was this. I answered it, as above, with the small but significant difference that I had suggested a reasonable level of allowance: you know, a couple of farthings and a tallow candle every other year, if the child was good. But Elinor, who had obviously been brought up in the lap of luxury compared to my humble beginnings, and more to the point was a staffed member of the *Telegraph* rather than an impoverished freelance and besides hadn't any children (then – I bet she's changed her tune now) thought the amount I suggested was stingy and quadrupled it to the vastly inflated, absurd figures, above.

I was appalled, hid the column as soon as I saw it, and made sure my children never clapped eyes on it. And as soon as I could, the next time Elinor went on holiday I expect, I redressed the balance.

DEAR ANNE – My parents have recently suggested giving me a monthly allowance, out of which I would have to pay for my entertainment and buy all my own clothes and shoes. What is the average allowance for a 14-year-old girl in my situation? Please reply soon, because my parents won't give me any money until they see your answer.
Sarah Jones, Cheshire

How about several hundred pounds a week, with a 10 per cent commission to the Agony Aunt who persuades your parents to part with it?

I've asked a number of 14-year-olds, and they say their allowances depend very much on what they are expected to buy.

For what it's worth, our own 14-year-old gets £14 a month. Out of this, she is expected to purchase any luxuries she wants: bus fares to friends' houses, Christmas and birthday presents, and gratuitous packets of Philadelphia cream cheese.

She doesn't have to pay for anything I consider important: music lessons, proper shoes and servicing her bicycle. She is also expected to give 10 per cent away, either to our church or to a charity.

I suggest you ask your parents to pay for your shoes, which are expensive, and get them to start you on £7 a week. You can find stylish outfits in markets and charity shops for next to nothing; Oxfam clothes have even been featured on *The Daily Telegraph*'s fashion page.

Give the first 70 pence to charity, put another £1 into a savings account and spend the rest as you wish. Review the situation regularly with your parents, tell them if it's not enough … and if it's too much, don't breathe a word. (Just send me a little something at Christmas. A £50 Unwins voucher would be ample.)

See? Perfectly reasonable. Having solved it, I then forgot all about this particular dispute.

Then last summer holidays, I employed my son Benjamin as my secretary for a few days to help catalogue the column preparatory to editing it for this book. As luck and the wheel of fortune would have it, the very first extract he read happened to be the first of these two letters (from B.S.) about levels of allowances.

He didn't bother to read any further. Nor did he believe any of my protestations or excuses. It turned out to be a very expensive few days.

Kind, loving parents have always tended have money worries. They also worry about their teenagers' social lives.

DEAR ANNE – My 16-year-old daughter has an assisted place at a private school. This has never caused us problems before; although many of the other girls have far more money, she gets on well with them and enjoys a superb education.

However, she has been invited to a black tie charity ball. As well as the ticket, we will need to buy her a gown. What can we do?

Mrs R.P., Oxfordshire

If you can possibly afford it, buy the ticket: feeling excluded is miserable. She could contribute a small sum towards it herself and perhaps grandparents can help, too. If the ball is hosted by the school, have a quiet word with the bursar (who will know your financial situation) and ask whether you can pay less for the ticket.

But there is no need for you to invest in a new frock. Encourage your daughter to trawl charity shops and jumble sales, or ask friends to lend her something.

The younger you are, the easier it is to improvise with clothes and still look terrific.

DEAR ANNE – My 15-year-old wants to have his first 'teenage' party. My friends think I'm mad, but he is responsible and well-mannered, and I think his good behaviour should be rewarded. However, the last thing I want is for it to get out of hand, and have all my friends saying 'I told you so'. Have you got any advice?

Mrs J.H., York

Find out what kind of party he wants. He might like a smart dinner party which you and your husband help to host. This isn't every teenager's cup of tea, but it's terrific fun – especially for you. If he prefers loud music, warm beer and dim lighting, you need clear rules. For instance: no uninvited guests, no one upstairs, no disturbing the neighbours. There should be a definite finishing time, with sensible travel arrangements home. Preferably no spirits and, obviously, no drugs. He should also clear up. Tell him, if all goes well, he can have another next year.

And change your friends. Miserable old fossils.

Not all teenagers, I'm happy to say, worry about exams. Some have more wholesome, rounded neuroses – about siblings, image, culture, or a truly robust approach to learning.

DEAR ANNE – I hate family summer holidays. I have to be nice to my sister, help wash up and even talk to my parents. Yuk.
John Peterson (14), Cornwall

Keep cool. In the wink of an eye, you'll be back at school with the longest term of the year ahead of you – you lucky thing.

DEAR ANNE – I enjoy listening to the Spice Girls, but I get the impression that this is not a cool thing to do.
Dom Taylor, Chiswick

Correct.

DEAR ANNE – I'm very into classical music, but my friends all like Brit Pop. Is this unnatural?
A.H. (15), Dyfed

It sounds very unnatural. So unnatural I've never heard of it. Does it come in a bottle, or is it a disease? I suggest you get some normal friends who appreciate Monteverdi.

DEAR ANNE – I started reading The Hobbit when I was nine, and was delighted to reach page 100 recently. Do you think I should take speed reading lessons?
T. Singer (17), London

Here's a simple guide: this is not a long column. You are near the end. You started reading it on Friday. Now, ask yourself, 'Has the weekend been and gone?'

"But I'm still reading the question!"

8. An Old-fashioned Man-eating Tiger

Our house has always been overrun with far too many animals. Something to do with our eldest's being destined for veterinary science, possibly. And the fact that we lived in a real, drafty vicarage with proper Beatrix Potter mouseholes and rat-attics … so we needed cats to control the rodents, dogs to control the cats, little boys to control the dogs, and so on, like the old woman who swallowed a fly.

What seemed reasonable in our home, however, threatened to become uncontrollable on the page. For some reason that I never quite got a handle on, my column became a refuge for all sorts of undesirable forms of wildlife, particularly spiders.

DEAR ANNE – How does one stop a six-year-old boy from telling lies? He is a bright, sociable child, much loved by his parents and by us, his grandparents. We have tried persuasion, example, threats, jokes and ignoring him – but all to no avail. His fibs include telling a schoolfriend he has a tarantula and saying his daddy is a shoemaker. My daughter is becoming quite worried, because she never knows when to believe him. Please help.
Name and address supplied

Lying is very common, and many otherwise honest children go through a fibbing phase. It sounds as though you have done all the obvious things: consistently rewarding him when he doesn't lie; praising him when he owns up. Your daughter could also investigate some of his claims when she doesn't know whether he's telling the truth; this will be humiliating for him, so she should explain why it must be done: 'If you've told lies before, what you say has to be tested until everyone is sure you've become trustworthy.' Expose his mendacity whenever possible, and ensure there are consequences when he's found out (but not when he voluntarily confesses) by taking away pocket money or a longed-for treat.

However, both the examples you give suggest a need to feel important; a tarantula would give him great street cred, and having a shoemaker for a father probably

"Check out my website!"

sounds romantic when you're six. Perhaps he doesn't have many friends, or they don't think much of him, and this is his way of getting more respect. If you can boost his self-confidence, he may not feel the need to embellish.

Even more intriguingly, it's possible that he's not really being dishonest at all, in the true sense of the word. Perhaps he's not lying (trying to deceive) so much as storytelling (trying to entertain). He may be wonderfully imaginative; a future Roald Dahl or Charles Dickens. I suggest you help him to write his stories down, and praise him for his fantastic inventiveness. If you give him a legitimate framework for making things up, he may no longer have any desire to deceive.

DEAR ANNE – Your letter about children lying reminded me of a friend who told her fibbing daughter that one could write a (true) letter to tell someone about what really happened, or tell a (false) story called 'picturesque imagination'. Soon, the child could be asked: 'PI or really true?' and she usually gave the right answer.
R.S., Tonbridge

DEAR ANNE – Re the small boy who tells lies … years ago, we told our son that his nose went red every time he lied. After that, he would hold his nose when lying. Our son is now telling his son the same story. Mrs J. Crown, Warwickshire

He's still lying, then?

I thought that was the end of it, but the tarantula had got its little hooks into my column, and was stealing a march on me.

DEAR ANNE – Last week, you suggested that a small boy might find a tarantula good for his ego. I gave a 10-year-old a tarantula this Christmas and it proved the ultimate gift – exciting, slightly frightening, and unusual; but also accommodating, quiet, unsmelly, unwalkable and fed only every other day (live crickets, with locusts for Sunday lunch). It caused a sensation at school. I can supply information about buying, housing and feeding these delightful pets. K.P., Bracknell

DEAR ANNE – I have a 10-year-old boy who read about the pet tarantula and has now got his heart set on having one. Can you help? P. T., Sudbury

DEAR ANNE – I'd love to have details about buying, housing and feeding tarantulas for my nine-year old granddaughter.
R.G., Crawley

I'm sure tarantulas make lovely pets, but I'd rather had enough of them.

Any more tarantula queries please, to Kit Pyman, c/o Features, *Daily Telegraph*, not to me. (Though, personally, I can't see what's wrong with a good old-fashioned man-eating tiger.)

I can't for the life of me now remember who Kit Pyman was, c/o Features, *Daily Telegraph*, nor why the queries were to be sent to him. But it sounds an excellent idea. I suggest anyone reading this who wants to talk about tarantulas should do the same. I'm sure Kit would be thrilled. In fact, write to anyone you like. Just don't mention them to me.

DEAR ANNE – I know you didn't want to hear any more about tarantulas, but you might like to investigate a recent discovery. When angered, tarantulas rub their legs together and produce a fine mist that can cause permanent eye damage.
J.S., London SW20

Oh my life: I had gone and promoted a highly dangerous animal that was going to blind half the nation's children.

Today's British Medical Journal carries an article on eye disease associated with handling pet tarantulas. It is now well documented that many of the so-called harmless American tarantulas – including the popular and widely available Chilean Rose – have developed special hairs to use against predators. These hairs can get into the eye and work their way through it, causing inflammation and permanent damage. Blue Peter mentioned this on Monday, saying that the risk is very slight, but three people have already had their eyes harmed. So, to be safe,

"It's called a Chilean Rose – just don't try smelling it!"

don't handle tarantulas routinely, don't let children pick them up or put their faces near them, use gloves and goggles when handling, and wash your hands afterwards. Above all, never annoy your tarantula. Our daughter bought a garter snake last week. These are charming creatures and pose a threat only to tadpoles.

I've just realized who Kit Pyman was, c/o the *Daily Telegraph* Features page. Not some poor beleaguered junior journalist, or Sixth Former on work experience who had been delegated the task of researching the wretched arachnids. No, he must have been the innocent correspondent, K.P. from Bracknell, who made the mistake of offering to supply information. He's probably left the country by now, or committed suicide under the weight of readers' letters.

So he won't suffer if you send him any more queries you might otherwise have been tempted to think of directing my way.

DEAR ANNE – I know you want no more information about tarantulas, but did you know that, on average, we swallow three spiders a year in our sleep?
L.W., Shropshire

I'm gripped. Who on earth researched that? And more to the point, *why?*

DEAR ANNE – Following your comment last Friday, I can't see anything wrong with a good old-fashioned man-eating tiger. Can you tell me where I can get one?
M.V. Lloyd, Hampshire

I could, but I've become rather shy of recommending nice furry pets.

By this time, I sympathised deeply with this next correspondent.

DEAR ANNE – I have a phobia about spiders. Whenever I think there's one near me, I start screaming and shouting. They are so ugly, I can't even look at them. Now, people are calling me a baby. Help! What shall I do?
Lucy Hurren (aged 11), London SW

First, bear in mind that arachnophobia is very common. I've seen a burly, 16-stone workman reduced to a jelly by a creature not much bigger than a pinhead. You can try to desensitize yourself by buying a plastic spider, or a picture of a real one, which you can then hold and learn to stroke. Next, use a more realistic, toy furry spider. Then, ask a friend or relative to tell you when there is an unthreatening little money spider nearby, so you can get used to it at a safe distance.

And so on. With each new step you will feel initial anxiety: it is important that you wait until you have calmed down, rather than running away immediately. If your phobia is so serious that it is disrupting your life, your GP can arrange for you to see a child psychiatrist. Alternatively you can buy a spider scoop to catch and deposit them in the garden. The Katcha Bug is very inexpensive, and available from www.plumcreekmarketing.com

---

Like my correspondents' letters, my answers were frequently cut down to fit the space (which varied according to the size of the advert on the page). This was true of my next answer; I had originally gone on to say that I had my dog put down, but my editor thought this was not important.

DEAR ANNE – My family's dog has not long to live. As my sister and I have left home, our parents will have to deal with her slow demise. Strangely, I feel more protective of them than of the dog, who has lived a long and much-adored life. I'm not sure they will be able to cope when she finally dies. Much as I will miss the dog, I feel I need to prepare myself more for my parents' loss, and a stark, dogless Christmas. What do you suggest?
F.D., London, W8

Allow yourself – and your parents – the grief appropriate to the occasion. It is normal to be broken-hearted. I, too, have had to listen to my dying dog howl through the night. But do remember she is only a dog. Your parents must feel free to say goodbye if she dies before Christmas, and then enjoy the festivities without feeling guilty. If she is no longer living a happy, fulfilled life, her death may even come as a relief to them.

And don't ever try to replace her. Get another pet by all means, but don't expect it to be the same. It never is.

But the extract that had been cut obviously had been important:

DEAR ANNE – As a dairy farmer, I was horrified and appalled to read that you let your dying dog 'howl through the night'.
Surely you should have taken him to the vet to be put down.
J.R., Surrey

I did, the very next day. He howled for one night. I howled for years.

Writing a column like this is a great education. I often researched and discovered things I would otherwise never have known.

DEAR ANNE – Last week, a bird flew up to the middle of one of our windows and pecked at the glass wildly in an attempt to come inside. I was so upset about the incident that I drew the curtains. However, when we returned home after a two-day absence, the bird was still trying to break the glass. Although I'm not an expert bird-watcher, I believe that it is a chaffinch. I'm worried that it will get hurt. What can I do?
C.B., Cambridgeshire

The bird is not trying to get in, but to attack the 'rival' it sees reflected in the glass. It is probably a young male bird without a mate, and can't understand why the other 'bird' is trespassing on its territory and won't back down. This is quite a problem at this time of year, especially with large birds such as swans. The only solution is to break up the reflection by sticking something on the outside of the glass. Clingfilm on the outer surface often works, or you might have to resort to newspaper. The good news is that once the birds start breeding, they will – like young humans – become far too busy to tilt at windmills. By May or June, this macho chaffinch will have better things to do.

And sometimes, I test-ran certain products on behalf of readers.

DEAR ANNE – I live in an area surrounded by cats. I love animals, but the way they torment and destroy songbirds distresses me. I am sure there was far more birdsong when I was a child than there is now. Is there anything I can do to help these birds?
A.S., Wembley

The decline of songbirds probably has as much to do with the destruction of hedgerows and increased use of pesticides as with predatory cats. Buying organic fruit and vegetables may do as much to help the songbird population as banning cats from your lawn, though it's a good idea to ask your cat-owner neighbours to keep their cats indoors in April and May, when the birds are breeding.

If your garden is small, you could try to prevent the cats from coming in by putting up Prickler Strip from the Network Pest Control (0151 4224838 www.network-pest.com) around the walls.

Or use the harmless sonic deterrent Dazer (01733 315888 www.dazer.com) as recommended by the Royal Society for the Protection of Birds, the Royal Horticultural Society and the Natural Trust. It is supposed to be effective even in a large and rambling garden.

I don't now know why I said this, because I tried it and it did absolutely nothing in our large and rambling garden. I put one under our doo'cot where I was breeding beautiful ornamental frill backs, Indian fantails, gorgeous pink and white feathered adornments to our garden, and my children's beastly cats continued to eat the stupid creatures all, one by one.

DEAR ANNE – I have always liked to think of myself as an open-minded parent, and enjoy allowing my children to fulfil their dreams.

Unfortunately, this seems to have resulted in our house being turned into a menagerie. We now have two hamsters, a guinea-pig, rabbits, budgerigars, and a tom cat who sprays all over my best furniture. Any advice?
Kate Loss, Aberdeen

That's nothing. As well as all the above except the budgies (and best furniture) our house has also had snakes, rats, chickens, ducks, drakes, dogs, doves, bees and now a Great Dane. As you know, if you can't beat them, you should join them: get yourself a hungry Rottweiler.

DEAR ANNE – My daughter asked for a hamster for her birthday. My son has a cat, so I suspected I was asking for trouble when I agreed to buy her a pair of hamsters. However, she was delighted.

It is now a week later, and both hamsters are dead – one beheaded, the other eaten. My daughter was, of course, absolutely devastated, and I feel very guilty that I put her through such a trauma. What should I get her as compensation?
Jane Thompson, Kent

Nothing. There is no compensation for life. Your daughter knew the risks as well as you did, and you certainly didn't give her the wrong present. Painful though the lesson was, it will help her when she faces worse bereavements later in life.

Though it was a bit tough on the hamsters …

When this next letter appeared, there had been much talk in the press about Humphrey, the cat who lived in Number Ten Downing Street (named after Sir Humphrey Appleby in Yes Minister) who had recently gone missing ...

DEAR ANNE – A stray cat has just started visiting us (we have our own cats and cat flap). We don't mind, but wonder whether we should try to find his rightful owner. What should we do?
A. and P.B., London

Do not contact Downing Street.

Get him to purr his memoirs into a microphone. I will happily ghost-write them for a very modest commission.

Feed him all the cream and sardines in your larder. With luck, you might even bring down the government.

(Chance would be a fine thing.)

DEAR ANNE – My cleaning lady has taken to pruning my pot plants so savagely that there is almost nothing left. Her English is poor, so it is tricky to explain that I prefer them with the foliage on. Have you any ideas?
Brian Goodfellow, Tooting

Why not be a man and get a tank of scorpions or a pet python instead? Pot plants, indeed.

9. Tears in My Pillow

As I've already said, adultery proved a common topic. But more often the adulterers themselves were not the ones to write to me: an affair tends to be more of a party for those engaged in it. After all, if sin weren't enjoyable, it would be much easier to resist.

The pain was more often endured by others.

DEAR ANNE – Do you have any advice beyond 'see a counsellor' or 'see a solicitor' to help cope with being told that your husband, whom you still love deeply, is in love with your best friend? The hurt and agony are overwhelming, and the sense of shock has stopped me functioning coherently. How can one live with knowing they are together?
Name and address supplied

There are occasionally times when all we can do is endure. If you have lost a child, a limb, or a partner, what possible consolation can another person give you? You've just got to keep going from day to day, knowing that one day your pain will be less raw.

Help yourself as much as possible. Organize all the things you've always wanted to do but didn't because your husband was around. What about that trip across Egypt that he didn't fancy? Redesign the house exactly as you want. Join that evening class. Have a dinner party for all your girlfriends. Give yourself frequent treats and nights out with others: an evening of Victoria Wood would brighten me up at death's door. Above all, try to find someone worse off than you whom you can help. This will cheer you up, give you back some feelings of self-esteem, and improve someone else's lot into the bargain.

Don't let yourself get bitter, or give way to hatred. Your husband may get over his infatuation, and you may still have a future together. But you need to show patience and forbearance – and prove to yourself, as well as to everyone else, that you can, and will, live successfully without him.

DEAR ANNE – A word of hope to your correspondent whose husband is in love with her best friend (17 January). About 25 years ago, I was in a similar situation, with four children aged eight to fifteen. I can relate to her pain, because I thought I would die of a broken heart. I am now 65, and I have lived a happy, fulfilled life, choosing not to marry again, but branching out into a new career and rearing my children successfully – I think. I have nine grandchildren who are a joy. I have peace of mind and a genuine feeling of wellbeing. There is light at the end of the tunnel, although at times one has to fight to get there.
C.C., Glasgow

DEAR ANNE – After years of enduring my first husband's infidelities, I divorced him. I am now happily remarried and have four children, yet I still find it hard to shake off the legacy of suspicion, distrust and insecurity. I am always imagining that my second husband will eventually succumb to someone younger, slimmer and more attractive. How can I conquer these fears?
B.P., Marlborough

Past experiences can sometimes leave us with irrational worries, and these can be very debilitating. Subject your anxieties to rigorous reasoning. Bear in mind that there are plenty of faithful husbands in the world, as well as unfaithful ones. After your experiences with your first husband, I imagine you chose someone more reliable the second time around: is he really likely to run off with another woman?

And there is no need to feel so helpless. You can't do anything about your age, but you can stay slim and make yourself as attractive as possible. Are you fun to be with? Are you a good companion? A good lover? Do you still do all the things that made your husband fall in love with you in the first place? Ask him. Talk it over together.

There is very little which is absolutely certain in this world. The greatest shame would be not to enjoy your husband and children today, because of your fears that they might not be with you tomorrow.

DEAR ANNE – Recently, my husband of 10 years dropped a bombshell. He said he thought it 'only fair to tell me' that he had been having an affair for the past six months. As I had imagined that we had the perfect marriage, I was devastated. Now he wants a divorce. As a Roman Catholic, I have always been completely opposed to divorce. When I said this, he accused me of

becoming pious to prevent him marrying the other woman. What should I do? Sacrifice my principles or ruin my husband's chance of happiness? I can't trust myself to decide, because I'm afraid my husband might be right when he says I'm being selfish.
Name and address supplied

And he is being a model of self-sacrifice, I suppose? The emotional blackmail he is subjecting you to is outrageous. If you don't want a divorce because you believe it to be wrong, don't give in to his demands: it is not ever fair for another human being to ask you to do something you believe to be morally wrong. If you want to preserve your marriage, feel free to fight for it with every fibre of your being. Under our present laws, you can't stop it happening for ever, but you can postpone the evil day.

Tell him that, for six months, you want him to stop seeing his mistress, attend counselling with you and give your relationship a real, whole-hearted try. Say you will not even discuss divorce until you have both done everything you can to save the marriage.

Aim to find out what made him want the other woman in the first place. Were you not spending enough time together? Was he sexually frustrated? Are there money worries? Is he lacking in confidence? Does he want children? Try to provide what he needs to make him happy – within your marriage. Don't feel guilty, don't be bullied and don't give up until you have to.

DEAR ANNE – Occasionally, I read in Agony Aunt columns that an affair can strengthen a marriage. Just under seven years into our marriage, my husband began a relationship with my so-called best friend. He found he could constantly lie to me and get away with it. Although he decided against leaving me and our four children, I suffered a mental breakdown, learnt to survive and realized that I could never trust him or respect him again.
Name supplied, Devon

Anyone who thinks cheating, lying and the breaking of promises strengthens a relationship is living in a fantasy world more bizarre than the one Alice found in her looking glass. Of course, in the initial, exciting boost to the confidence which comes with any new romance, an adulterer often feels he or she can cope better with everything – including the hard slog of marriage. The day of reckoning comes later – and, sadly, it is often the innocent spouse or the children who suffer.

I suggest you ask yourself, and your husband, how you are going to change your relationship so that you can trust and respect him again. You should tell him how much he has hurt you and warn him that he cannot repeat such behaviour. But you also need to forgive him. He is responsible for his affair: you are responsible for your resentment. It is this which is now ruining your life.

God can always bring good out of evil; after all, beautiful poetry blossomed in the trenches of the Great War. Adultery is never recommended; but make the best of what you have now. It is possible, in the reconciliation and forgiveness that can follow an affair, for a marriage eventually to emerge sadder but wiser.

Sometimes it was hard to tell which broken-hearted victim of adultery the letter was from.

DEAR ANNE – If parents really love their children, how can they possibly contemplate, or have, a long-standing affair without realizing the hurt and damage it will cause to their family? I would appreciate your advice.
Name and address withheld

Because none of us loves perfectly.

I believe the Prince of Wales loves his children, as did the late Princess. But I confess I was surprised to hear her described as a flawless mother. In many ways she undoubtedly was a wonderful parent – as he still is. But I would not consider it conventional good parenting to go on prime time television and publicize one's extramarital affairs. I don't suppose their sons particularly appreciated their friends knowing that their parents didn't love them enough to love each other.

Let's be honest: just as our sincerest laughter with some pain is fraught, so our sincerest love with selfishness is spoilt. We are all guilty. I do, genuinely, love my children. And yet I keep losing my temper with them, though I know it hurts and damages them. And although I know it's wrong.

Undoubtedly your pain is in a different league. You ask for advice. I'm not sure whether you are telling me about your parent or your partner. Either way, tackle the one who is having the affair, and say, in no uncertain terms, that the behaviour is wrong and not worthy of a loving parent. You say there is a lack of realisation, so spell out the consequences. Describe the damage it does. Demand that it should stop. Don't give up.

But bear in mind that we all have failings – and that includes you and me.

DEAR ANNE – In the summer, my husband left me and our two small children to live with his mistress. This came as a shock both to me and to all my family.

My once kind and gentlemanly husband is now impulsive, unkind and irrational. His family is convinced that he has reached his mid-life crisis and say that he will eventually 'come to his senses'. However, I wonder if this is what they prefer to believe.

I took my marriage vows very seriously and, now, everything I believe in has been shattered. I have two questions for you. If you were in my position, what would you be praying for? And if he ever wanted to come back, would you have him?
Name and address supplied

You suggest I would do what I believe to be right, which is generous of you. But let's assume I would act rationally.

First, I would pray for myself: that I'd have the courage to resist self-pity, the strength to bring my children up on my own and the generosity to do so without bitterness. Then I would pray for them, hoping that they could continue to love their father, without condoning (or copying) his example when they are older.

If I had any energy left, I would pray that he would see sense, or that his mistress would get sick of him, or both – but I wouldn't count on this happening.

If it did, I would not have him back unconditionally. He would have to agree never to see or communicate with his mistress again, and repent pretty convincingly before I'd welcome him home. Then, however, I would genuinely try not to mention or even think of her again, so we could start afresh.

I do hope, for the sake of both of you and your children, that he wakes up and realizes his folly.

DEAR ANNE – I am a bachelor living alone, and my next-door neighbours are a lovely couple in their thirties, with three small children. They both work long and irregular hours, so they don't have much time together, except at weekends.

Last year, when she was pregnant, I noticed a young man visiting her in the mornings, often parking his car out of sight of the house. The visits stopped for a while after she gave birth, but have recently started again. On each visit, he stays for 20 to 30 minutes.

I daren't jump to conclusions or say anything to the husband because I don't know the facts. However, I do believe something untoward might be going on. Any advice you can give would be greatly appreciated.

H.S., Somerset

The most obvious explanation for the man's visits is that he is her doctor or midwife, and she is pregnant again. Indeed, if you know her well enough, you might ask her whether this is the case, so you can offer congratulations. (If there is something more sinister behind his visits, your polite inquiry might shock her into rethinking her priorities; but I think it's most unlikely that this is the case.)

It's much more worrying that they don't spend much time together. This can put a strain on any marriage, particularly when it is combined with the extra demands of a young family.

But you can't help them unless they know and trust you. Your concern does you credit: I suggest you also become better friends with them. Perhaps you could invite them over for drinks; or take him to the pub occasionally. Once you are considered a good friend, you can express any worries you have. Otherwise, you'll just seem plain nosy.

Occasionally I received a letter that baffled me. The next one haunted me. The pain that this correspondent was enduring had gone on and on. He was surely doing the right thing from a moral point of view, but his earthly reward was merely the thin gruel of unselfish frustration, weeping and loneliness.

For a long time I wondered whether my advice was of any use at all, whether he found the love of God, what had happened to his story ...

DEAR ANNE – Nine years ago, I fell passionately in love with a divorced friend; we could not cope with the deceit, so we ended our affair and I returned to being a faithful husband and father. I no longer think of myself as a Christian, but I do value Christian morals.

However, I cannot forget the true love I found so long ago. I hesitate to say that my marriage is a loveless one, but it has never inspired deep affection. I try to show my wife consideration; she sees our relationship as a safe haven and seems content.

For eight long years, I have thought daily of the woman with whom I am in love, and nightly shed tears in my pillow. Is this what God wishes? I am not the husband my wife deserves, I have failed the woman I love, and all I can do is watch as three lives slip away without fulfilment.

Name and address supplied

I don't need to tell you what the Christian morality, which you value, is. You clearly know it as well as I do. The Bible tells you to delight in the wife of your youth (Proverbs 5:18, 19). And, as a general rule, this leads to greater happiness: countless men have felt as you have, and left wives for mistresses, only to find – after a year or two – that the excitement, fulfilment and noble sentiments inevitably give way to the tedium of everyday chores, but without shared early memories and secure and contented children. There is no guarantee that if you had your freedom you would find fulfilment.

But I must be honest. It's possible you would: you might well be happier if you were living with the woman you love. No one can tell. In your case, it sounds quite likely. Your children would be devastated, your wife would weep, but if this life is all you have, you must presumably live it the best you can – which may mean being selfish.

The point is that Christian morality only makes sense in the context of a relationship with Christ. The end of Christianity is not that it always makes us happier here and now, but that we will be happier one day; that we can throw this life away for others, because Another threw His life away for us; that we can afford to waste this existence, because we have another so much better to look forward to. If the promise is one of Eternity, we can cope more easily with the sorrow of a few decades that are less than they might be.

So I believe there is a far more important issue at stake here: that of your lost faith. Lose your love for Jesus, and you lose everything: the reason behind Christian morality, its purpose and its reward. Find this, and the rest of your life would eventually begin to fall into place.

You ask what God wishes. I believe He wishes – nay, longs – for you to find your hope, your fulfilment, your salvation in Him.

I assumed I was destined never to know what happened, as with most of my correspondents. But years later, in response to the standard letter I sent out to all my correspondents asking for permission to publish their letters again, I received this.

You offered me advice that I thought both sensible and sensitive. In fact, I was very grateful indeed, first to have been able to share my agonizing dilemma with someone else, especially someone so positive (certainty is a great comfort to the waverer!). Second, you gave me the direction that I knew in my heart was right.

And so I wrote you a follow-up letter to express my appreciation. I wondered then if you received it, but it sounds, sadly, as if you did not.

You are naturally interested in the impact of your advice. Sorry I cannot report anything dramatic or amusing, only that I continued to pine for my lost 'real love' until I received from her a contemptuous,

stinging rebuke for my inactivity. This largely deflated the unquestioning devotion and blind love I had felt, when I saw that, for her, possessing a husband was more important than the romantic love I had cherished.

And so I resigned myself with better spirit to my marriage that has many advantages to compensate for the lack of passion. As you pointed out, passion with a new woman might not endure either!

I do my best to share my thoughts, feelings and enthusiasms with my wife. I sometimes long for a woman I can embrace and enfold with the infinite love that wells up from time to time, but I suppose we all have our cross to bear ...

Could such a satisfied client possibly object to publication? Of course not. I would feel honoured.

He enclosed the letter he had written several years before, which I had never received.

Please accept these sincere thanks from me, after you answered my question so wisely. I had no difficulty recognizing myself from the masterly précis of my letter.

I can well believe that if I could fully restore my Christian faith, it would fill my spiritual need. But the world is full of people who cannot focus their deepest emotions on an invisible deity, and for them, I feel sure, Nature has ordained mortal love instead. Perhaps it is after all a form of faith that will not allow me willingly to hurt anyone; certainly not my companion of 28 years.

Your response was perceptive and sympathetic. I shall think about it for a very long time, and it will continue to influence my thinking. If it can also help others, as it surely will, it is very satisfying.

Thank you again, dear Anne.

10. Turn the Other Cheek

A few months before I was invited to become an agony aunt, I had begun doing Thought for the Day on Radio 4's Today Programme: this had, in turn, led to more freelance journalism, from which sprang the column. In some ways this made my job much easier: I had come to the editor's attention because of these brief Christian broadcasts, so I felt I had been employed as a Christian and was expected to give a Christian response.

Nonetheless I fleetingly wondered – as I suppose all Christians do, in one way or another, when considering their careers – whether I should try to make my job secure before making too much of a Christian stand. Initially, the column was to run for a trial period of three months; should I 'soft pedal' on my faith for that time, in the hope that the work would be extended? It took only a moment's reflection to see how daft and illogical this would be. At the time the *Telegraph* was selling over a million copies, which meant a readership of two and a half million. Suppose my job was only ever destined to be for those three brief months and no more: how would I answer God, on the Day of Judgment, when He said: 'I gave you a readership of two and a half million people, for three long months, and you didn't tell them the Gospel'?

So I decided to be as outspoken as I could, in case I only had that little time to speak. (In the end, the column ran for over three years.)

DEAR ANNE – Operating from within the security of your religious faith, you may not appreciate the agonies of people who are not protected in this way. I am not against faith – it would have helped me a lot – but how is it achieved? My local Church of England vicar is about as spiritual as a bank manager. When I asked him this question, he squirmed and suggested I consult a Catholic priest. How do I find the kind of faith that would help me in the face of life's adversity?
A.K., Milton Keynes

The Church traditionally recognizes three ways to develop faith: scripture, prayer and fellowship. Have confidence in the Scriptures; they are outstandingly reliable by any standards (see, for instance, Craig Blomberg's *The Historical Reliability of the Gospels*, IVP, or Paul Barnett's *Is the New Testament History?* Hodder Christian Paperbacks). Read Luke again: he specifically wrote his Gospel so we could have certainty in our faith. Try to study the Bible every day. Ask God for faith. He promises that if we seek Him with all our heart, we will find Him (Jeremiah 29:13). Pray regularly. And finally, find a church where the Gospel is preached, so you can get encouragement from other Christians. Try St Mary's, Bletchley (telephone: 01908 366531 www.st-marys-bletchley.org), which is near you. I rang the curate there and asked how he would answer your question, and he had plenty of suggestions. (Alternatively, perhaps your vicar's advice was the best he's ever given ...)

(Bear in mind that the *Telegraph*'s editor, Charles Moore – whom I liked and admired enormously, and who was my boss, when all's said and done – had recently converted to Catholicism.)

DEAR ANNE – A few weeks ago, someone wrote and asked you how she could keep her faith fresh and you advised her to read St Luke. So, after years of neglecting my Bible, I read St Luke, too, and was gripped. I would now like to read what others have written about the Gospels and Jesus – particularly the parables. B.S., Gerrards Cross

Dorothy Sayers's introduction to her play-cycle *The Man Born to be King* is brilliant, but you'll have to scour the second-hand bookshops because it's out of print. Meanwhile, try the series called *The Jesus Library* (Hodder & Stoughton) – particularly *The Parables of Jesus* by David Wenham. For a more novelistic approach, read Gerd Theissen's *The Shadow of the Galilean* (SCM Press).

Best of all, since you enjoyed Luke so much, remember that, in the style of all best-selling authors, he wrote a sequel, the Acts of the Apostles ...

I liked to include one question about faith in each column. Happily, there was no shortage of interesting queries.

DEAR ANNE – You have been quoted as saying that 'to be an atheist is the worst sin'. Is it true? Did you say this? I am an atheist and my thoughts are based on 50 years of search, inquiry, study and feeling. If what you are saying is correct, then I am worse than a child molester or a murderer. How should I deal with that? Alan Ross, Sussex

Sin is a technical theological word. It means independence from God, and is first depicted in the Bible by two people merely eating fruit. This is hardly shocking, after-the-watershed stuff, but it was contrary to God's instructions. So sin is not primarily anti-social behaviour – the confusion arises because anti-social acts are also contrary to God's instructions. If God exists, then the purpose of man, in the words of the catechism, is 'to glorify God and enjoy Him forever'. Sin cuts us off from Him. Ignoring Him (whether such ignorance is voluntary or not) sep-

arates us from Him more effectively than any other 'sin' we might commit.

But your question is surprising: surely sin only presents a problem to a believer. You have spent 50 years concluding that God doesn't exist. Provided you are right, there is nothing to worry about.

It's just not a gamble I'm prepared to take.

DEAR ANNE – Why is today called Good Friday? Shouldn't it be Bad Friday?
Hannah Thompson, aged seven

Ask your grandparents to tell you about the Battle of Britain, and then ask them whether they thought it was a good or a bad time. For those fighting – and their friends and relations – it must have been an awful period to live through. But for the rest of us, looking back, it was a great time. After all, it was when Britain more or less won the war and secured the freedom that we've all enjoyed ever since. Although it was a bad experience at the time for those who were there, the long-term consequences were very good.

Good Friday was the same. It

was bad that 'commonplace human beings ... killed and murdered God Almighty' (as Dorothy Sayers described the Crucifixion), but, in the long term, it was very good for us that God let them do it. For Jesus, His mother and friends, it must have been terrible.

I cannot begin to imagine how frightening it was for Jesus Himself when He realized that God had abandoned Him. However, the moment when God forsook Jesus was the moment when He took all our sins away – which makes it, for you and me, the very best day in the entire history of the world.

DEAR ANNE – I have been asked to be a godfather to a friend's son. Although I am a believer in God, I do not take part in organized religion, nor am I particularly demonstrative. However, I am keen to accept. Is there anywhere I can learn what my duties are, and what my role should be?
Name and address supplied

Yes: in the Book of Common Prayer.

Being a godparent is a great privilege but also an awesome

responsibility. First, you must be baptized and confirmed yourself. You will need to make public statements and vows about your faith, which you will find (along with a godparent's duties) in the Prayer Book. If you cannot say those comfortably, I would urge you to decline, and ask instead if you could be a secular sponsor for the child.

In the baptism service, you will be asked if you believe and trust in the Father, Son and Holy Spirit, and if you are prepared to renounce the world and obey God's commandments for the rest of your life. You will be required to answer publicly, and then charged to ensure that the child is brought up in the faith until he is old enough to answer for himself at his confirmation. In practice, this means praying for him regularly, making sure he attends church, understands Christianity, reads his Bible and learns to pray.

There are no secular duties, but to do the above properly you will not only need to make a commitment to Christianity yourself, but also build a deep and lasting relationship with your godson. The best guide is common sense. Most children appreciate trips to a sticky bun shop or to the zoo as well as to church. Also, your time will be worth far more to him than money or presents. And, rather than just sending something for his birthday or Christmas (which everyone does), remember his baptism anniversary, too.

DEAR ANNE – Every year my godfather sees Easter as his chance to convert me back to the Catholic faith of my childhood. I am happy to go with him to Mass and to meet the priests, but I feel I am wasting their time.

I do not feel drawn toward the Church except as a haven of tradition. I understand that Catholicism has brought him solace in his later years, but I do not feel the pull myself and dread these attempts to save my soul. He would be terribly hurt if I squashed his evangelistic attempts, but they create an uncomfortable tension between us.
I.H., Wimbledon

If you enjoy Mass and like meeting the priests, I'm puzzled as to why you dread his efforts. I'm sure they don't resent spending time with you, since the purpose of Christians on this Earth is to tell others the Good News, and priests are set aside to do this full-time.

I suggest you tell them you are unconvinced by the Christian argument, and give them a chance to debate with you: all the Catholic clergy I know would relish the challenge.

I doubt if your godfather will mind if you tell him your honest feelings, while still having the good manners to accompany him.

DEAR ANNE – As a churchwarden, I agree with your recent comment that godparents must be believers. If only the clergy would be so unequivocal. I read recently that the General Synod is proposing that, at infant baptism, parents and godparents should not be asked to make public statements about their faith. Whatever next?
L.B.B., Harrogate

I dread to think. Mind you, it wouldn't be the silliest thing Synod has considered in recent years.

Some questions were not about faith itself, but asking for a Christian response to a particular dilemma.

DEAR ANNE – I would like to think that I am a Christian, although the Good Lord may disagree. I want to join the local Territorial Army Reserve unit, but can a man be both a Christian and a soldier? Also, TA exercises take place on Sunday. Should I take part in a Sunday activity for which I would be paid?
R.C., Cheltenham

You raise two interesting questions about which Christians generally agree to disagree. My father could not in conscience fight in the war, although his best friend, who was also a Christian, was compelled by his conscience to do so (and gave his life). They loved and respected each other greatly, although they disagreed passionately. Article 37 of the Book of Common Prayer states: 'It is lawful for Christian men ... to wear weapons, and serve in the wars.' Yet many non-conformists, for instance Mennonites and Quakers, believe that Christians should be pacifists.

Similarly, Eric Liddell (of *Chariots of Fire* fame) was a Christian athlete who wouldn't run on a Sunday, even as an amateur. Yet plenty of Christian policemen, clergy, nurses and others providing less essential services do paid work on Sundays. There are no easy answers. Decide what you think is right, not what is convenient. Read C.S. Lewis's essay 'Why I Am Not a Pacifist' in *Timeless At Heart* (Collins). Also read Part II of *Issues Facing Christians Today* by John Stott (Marshall), which has sections on pacifism and 'the just war'. Work out when you would have Christian fellowship and teaching if you train on Sunday: can you join a midweek group?

And, with reference to your first sentence, put your faith in what Christ has done for you, not what you do for Him – so you don't get a nasty surprise when the trumpet sounds.

DEAR ANNE – As a Christian bachelor, I am fed up with unrequited love and sexual frustration. When I was recently made redundant, I felt that God was closing my door to marriage for good. How can I be released from this mental prison?
Name supplied, Wimbledon

It's not easy, but since you believe in God, you presumably believe He knows best. If marriage would really be better for you, redundancy won't be a problem to Him. Why not give Him a helping hand? A married couple in our previous church met through a Christian dating agency. Try New Day Introductions (Tel: 01706 224049 www.marriageintroductions.co.uk).

In the meantime, read Paul (1 Corinthians 7) to remind yourself of all the advantages you have over married people: be thankful for the freedom God has given you now. It may be frustrating, but it isn't half as frustrating as an unhappy marriage.

Coincidentally, the vicar of your local church is an extremely sexy bachelor whom I have known since I was at school. He must have had dozens of offers, not all of them quite proper – and several of them from me, as far as I can recall – but has resisted them all. I asked him how he coped, and he said cold baths are very under-rated. I suggest you pitch up one Sunday morning and ask for sensible pastoral advice. Emmanuel Church, The Ridgeway, Wimbledon, Sundays 11 a.m. (www.wimbledon.org.uk)

DEAR ANNE – I am shocked at what you say about your sexy bachelor vicar friend and his suggested use of 'under-rated' cold baths to help with the frustration of being single. Doesn't he know there is a water shortage?
P.C., Leicester

Don't worry; my friend is pretty stoical, so I wouldn't be surprised to hear that he uses the same bath water for months on end.

Some of the questions sent to me were downright nuts. So daft, in fact, that I didn't publish them – though on this next occasion I referred to a couple. Bear with me: it does all have a tenuous connection with Christianity, if you read on. (And in response to your next question: no, I absolutely did not make them up. I'm not that creative.)

DEAR ANNE – Do you have any views on naturism? Is it possible to have a positive approach to nakedness, either in the family or in a naturist environment?
P. James, Birmingham

I have a very positive approach to nakedness within the family, though my children are more squeamish; I put this down to two neurotically prudish au pairs we had once. The trouble with naturists, though, is that we'd all like them to look like Elle Macpherson or Brad Pitt, but in fact they have the same saggy bits and cellulite as the rest of us.

A few years ago, the mayor of an Italian resort had the excellent idea of making it illegal for ugly people to strip off. Beautiful young girls were allowed to: hideous old hags were not. This is exactly the right approach in my view. Unfortunately, in egalitarian England we would go into paroxysms of politically correct paranoia before passing such an obviously sensible by-law.

So, on balance, I think it best to keep nudity within the family, or when bathing with members of the same sex.

DEAR ANNE – I must take issue with your answer to P. James' inquiry on naturism (15 May).

I have been a member of a naturist club for ten years, and I can assure you that most of us have no wish to look like Elle Macpherson or Brad Pitt. P. James should contact the Central Council for British Naturism, which will supply details of the naturist movement and local clubs.
Penny Stephens, London N16

I don't know if it's because of the warmer weather, but my correspondents seem to have become obsessed with various states of undress. I have also received a letter from someone whose deaconess dances naked in the church aisle, and another from a woman who wonders whether her vicar will mind if she is baptized in the altogether.

Naturism: a time and a place!

DEAR ANNE – I wonder if you could help me with a problem that is bothering me considerably. Although I am a normal 21-year-old girl in every respect, I've always enjoyed wearing a shirt and tie. I don't wear them all the time, but am really pleased when I do, as I think I look smart.

However, I often wear the tie with a skirt, and am constantly teased by my friends at work, who accuse me of 'cross dressing'. My boyfriend says he thinks my dress sense is fine – he even gave me a tie for my birthday. Is this really such a strange thing to do? Shall I give up the habit, or persevere?
S.R., Shropshire

Persevere, definitely. I'd be prepared to bet that these 'friends' are either girls who are jealous of your dress sense, or men threatened by your competence.

Women have always looked attractive when subtly imitating certain aspects of men's fashion. Take a glance at Victorian riding habits, ties worn by Edwardian women above beautiful long skirts, or jodhpurs and jackboots. Some ideas don't work: women look jolly silly in clerical dog-collars – but then again, so does any man under 60 years of age.

All this is very different from cross-dressing, which is an attempt to be mistaken for a member of the opposite sex.

Your boyfriend is right; your colleagues are wrong; and you should wear what you please.

DEAR ANNE – I must take issue with your recent statement that women look jolly silly in clerical dog-collars. Many female ministers in the Methodist church wear clerical collars and look extremely dignified and attractive.
F.J. Robertson, Orpington

I believe I can claim more friends in dog-collars than the average agony aunt and, I assure you, the only people who don't look ridiculous in them are men born before 1930. Cassocks, though, are a different matter.

SIR – I have to disagree with Anne Atkins's recent claim that only gentlemen born before 1930 look good in dog collars.

My 28-year-old husband, a curate in the Church in Wales (shown in the photograph, below) looks extremely good in his. So do many of his colleagues who were all born well after 1930.
Kirsten Gable, Porthcawl, S. Glamorgan

This last was unfair. You can hardly say what you think of the sex appeal (or lack of it) of another woman's husband. It was on the tip of my pen to question the taste of any woman who chooses a man in a beard, let alone a dog collar ... but some bright spark would have written back to say that Jesus had a beard; to which the obvious reply would be that Jesus also wore what looks to us like a dress, and you'd hardly want your husband in that – at which point half the vicar's wives in the country would have written to say their husbands wear dresses every Sunday ...

The clergy, of course, are always easy targets.

DEAR ANNE – Our priest regularly takes an hour and a quarter to say mass, and the numbers attending church are falling. I'm sure the two are connected. It's very wearing for those with children (and those around them).

We are all very busy and have little enough time these days. How can we make the clergy see that 'less is more'?
Mrs M., Orpington

Alas, your poor priest. A mass has a given number of words in it: do you want him to speak twice as fast, or give you Episode Two next Sunday?

Length is not the issue. Communion in our church (as abbreviated as is legal) is just as long, yet the congregation – including dozens of little children – stays for an hour afterwards drinking coffee. I presume this is because the time is well spent and interesting.

One difficulty is that modern Western children are no longer able to sit still. But the real problem, dare I say it, is yours: an attitude not of family membership but of consumerism. I suggest you canvass support from others, then approach your priest and offer to organize congenial and informative Sunday School activities during mass.

And bear in mind that, sometimes, less is less.

Talking of Roman Catholicism, I suspect it's time for my confession. But first, a couple from other people.

DEAR ANNE – I had always felt that it was wrong to pinch pens and other stationery from work and, until now, had always been punctilious about never doing this or making private telephone calls in office time. However, since all my colleagues seem to help themselves to whatever they want and ring their friends all the time, I have started to copy them. Is this wrong?
C.C., Leeds

Yes.

DEAR ANNE – I told my colleagues that I had given up chocolate for Lent, but I cheated. What do I do? Confess, or stay silent? J.T., East Sussex

Spit it out.

Now mine.

Living in a vicarage, one receives one's fair share of ghastly letters: neighbours complaining about children from the local nursery school playing in the garden; the church bell ringing at nine o'clock on a Sunday morning; bees going about their business from the vicarage bee hives; or the sound of chickens clucking gently in the vicarage flower beds. Once we had a note protesting at our cat's being pregnant, and one church-hater regularly wrote to us with complaints which always began with her age, as if that was our fault too.

One must, of course, always respond graciously … but it can be wearing on the professionalism of the most patient vicar.

Well, what is the point of being an Agony Aunt if you can't occasionally answer personal letters in your work time?

DEAR ANNE – I feel I must write to say how dismayed and disappointed I am every time I pass the ill kempt and slovenly garden of my local vicar. It is a real mess: the lawn unmown and the beds unweeded. Many years ago, I was a regular churchgoer; now I very rarely attend services. The scruffy appearance of my church does nothing to encourage me.
Mrs D.W., London SW6

I must congratulate you on the most original excuse I have ever heard: I would love to see St Peter's face when you tell him why you haven't been to church. Do you honestly believe that if your vicar were a better gardener you would go every week? Our church is typical in costing £10 per head per week to run (though many churchgoers in the country put a fiver in the collection box and think they are doing the church a favour, rather than realizing that they are being subsidized) and that certainly does not include hiring a

"Sorry, until you get that gate sorted out, I'm simply not coming in!"

gardener. Would you offer to visit the sick and elderly, to free your vicar for more important things such as mowing the lawn? Most clergy I know work longer hours than a doctor, for about a quarter of the pay. When do you think he has time to attend to the herbaceous border? I suggest you join the church immediately, since Jesus said He came for people just like you ... though I doubt that your vicar will thank me if you take my advice.

DEAR ANNE – I have the obvious answer to your correspondent D.W., who was too disgusted by her vicar's unmown lawn to go to church. She should join our congregation. Just before I read her letter, I had been cutting the grass outside our vicarage. This task used to take four hours, but when my husband developed a heart condition, we dipped into our frugal savings and bought a sit-on mower for £700. Now I can zoom round in half the time, while my husband fritters his days away visiting the sick and carrying out his parish duties. Do you think that if I cultivate twee flower beds around the garden, as well, I will persuade others who have fallen by the wayside to return to church? Give me strength!
Cynthia Taylor, The Vicarage, Haigh, Wigan

And recently:

DEAR ANNE – The interesting thing which arose from the appearance of my letter, was the fact that you published my full address, and through this I received a letter from the daughter of a former incumbent here at Haigh. She had fond memories of the garden. Margaret and I corresponded often and still exchange news at Christmas, so a friendship has been formed, courtesy of your column and Mrs D.W.'s complaints about her vicar's garden!
Cynthia Taylor, The Vicarage, Haigh, Wigan

PS Sadly I will soon have to leave this garden when my husband retires, though I am only in my fifties. The thought of not being able to live in the parish or worship in the church is very daunting ...

By then I, too, had had to leave behind our beloved garden that Mrs D.W. had complained about. (Though naturally, she was moaning about the front garden, which was only there to impress the neighbours. It was leaving the wonderful romantic back garden that caused the heartache.) I sympathize deeply with Mrs Taylor.

Another letter came from parishioners, in response to the following:

DEAR ANNE – I really fancy my geography teacher.
Miss X (13), St Paul's Girls' School

Well, your taste is certainly good. I've met him, too, and he's scrumptious. But he's the wrong age for either of us, so we'll just have to pull ourselves together.

So, the very next week:

DEAR ANNE – We really fancy our vicar.
Misses X, Y and Z, Parsons Green

Yeah, well, so do I. And he's spoken for, so hands off.

Questions about Christianity had their share of agony too. A guilty conscience is often the scourge of the spiritual life.

DEAR ANNE – After 39 years of marriage, I am about to seek a divorce. I have many faults, but have always been mindful of my vows and – under difficult circumstances – have been the best wife and mother I possibly could. Now I feel that it's all been for nothing. My husband has always been a gambler: that came first, before me, the children and the marriage. We have all suffered; my health – both physical and mental – is poor from all the stress (his is fine). The Bible says that 'a wife must put her husband first. This is her duty as a follower of the Lord. A husband must love his wife and not abuse her' (Colossians 3:18–19). Should I feel guilty about abandoning my duties to try to find a little happiness and a peaceful existence? I have been an absolute fool and time isn't on my side. But nothing in the future could be as bad as the past.
Mrs B., Hertfordshire

If you have decided on a particular course of action and you believe it is the right thing to do, don't feel guilty about your choice. A bad conscience can be a good thing: it can alert us to the fact that we are doing something wrong. But guilt can also be destructive, particularly if it is fuelled by low self esteem.

You are hard on yourself. Being a dutiful wife has not 'been for nothing'; it has given your children a stable home and you, presumably, have gained patience and self-discipline. You quote St

Paul, who says elsewhere that he is happy to be a 'fool for Christ' (1 Corinthians 4:10). As he shows us, it can be right to be foolish, to trust someone who isn't trustworthy, to 'waste' the best years of our lives for the sake of a promise made long ago. Be proud of your past: it may have felt pointless in terms of your marriage, but it won't have been wasted on your soul. As for the future, if you believe it is wrong to 'abandon your duties', then don't. But if you think it is right to go, don't feel guilty.

DEAR ANNE – About six months ago, my daughter, who has two small sons, left her husband to move in with a colleague who is himself married with young children. As Christians, my husband and I were greatly saddened by her behaviour. But we told her that although we disagreed with what she had done and didn't want to meet the other man, we loved her come what may.

We have prayed that the relationship might soon end, and have done our best to support our devastated son-in-law. Not surprisingly, my daughter has drifted away from God, which I find distressing since I believe that what we do here has eternal consequences.

Meanwhile, there may soon be talk of divorce and remarriage. My question is: what should our attitude be if the relationship continues? What is the truly Christian response?
Name and address supplied

Give your grandchildren and their father all the love and support you can. Your reaction so far has been exemplary. You are right to say there may be eternal consequences, the most serious of which is your daughter's drift from God. Her lover currently has a greater attraction for her than her Maker – a common problem. You must pray that whatever happens, she does not cut herself off from God completely.

Try to be a living example of His love, by showing her she will always be welcomed and accepted by you. She knows your view of her relationship, so you needn't reiterate your opinions. But she will need reminders of your love.

Your commitment to her means that if her affair continues and becomes formalized, it may be appropriate for you to meet the man. Try not to do anything now that might jeopardize a future relationship with him. I know some loving parents who expressed disapproval of their daughter's relationship with a married man; she has now been with him for more than 20 years and he still remembers the hurt their attitude caused.

DEAR ANNE – Recently, you answered a letter from parents deeply worried about the faith of their daughter, who had left her husband and children for another man and was no longer attending church.

Four years ago, I did the same. Please tell them that, however much she is blamed by them, privately she will blame herself far more. Any temporary departure from worship may be because she is feeling too guilty to pray or go to church. Most people who do such things are not naturally sinful, and are genuinely repentant – when it is too late! I have remarried, and my new husband and I have a wonderful relationship with my children. Our church is a central part of our lives: we attend regularly and sing in the choir together. We know how important it is to be forgiven.
S.H., Oxford

I have a friend whose story is so similar that I had to read your name several times to convince myself your letter hadn't come from her. It is clearly a common experience.

Sometimes though, one feels a bad conscience mightn't go amiss.

DEAR ANNE – My Jewish companion and I are in our late fifties and are both widowed. Since we live in different countries, we don't intend to get married, though we adore each other and make love frequently.

However, I am having trouble reconciling extra-marital sex with the teaching of the Church, and with being an active Christian.
C.B., Weymouth

I'm not surprised. You can't possibly reconcile the two.

The teaching of both the Church and the Torah, of scripture and Jesus Himself, is that sex is created to be enjoyed between people who are committed to one another for life – in other words, those who care more for each other than for their independence or their countries.

In addition, both Christianity and Judaism teach that you should aim to marry within your own faith. Why do you think you know better?

I said earlier that I usually vetoed the loonier questions. But both of these were pretty silly, and I still seem to have published them.

DEAR ANNE – Should one kneel to pray, or is sliding forward in the seat and bowing the head acceptable?
P.T., Hastings

Well, since 'God sees the heart', 1 Samuel 16:7 (which is in much the same place in either position), I don't suppose He cares much.

DEAR ANNE – I have a problem with my dust-buster vacuum cleaner. I used it to suck up some Parmesan cheese spilt by my toddler son Tristan and now it has very bad breath. As a Christian, what would you advise?
Mr A. Tatarek, Aldershot

As a Christian, I would advise kindness, compassion, and common sense. Before you use the vacuum cleaner again, sprinkle the carpet with Listerine.

Doing the shake and vac

Then we somehow embarked on an entire daft correspondence about the way the clergy spend their time.

DEAR ANNE – I am very interested in trains, especially fast ones, but my friends tell me I'm sad. Surely train-spotting is no worse than any other interest?
Joe Smiley, London

It all depends what you're comparing it with. Trainspotting isn't nearly as sad as being interested in Top Gear or Tamagotchis. But then that's not saying much.

DEAR ANNE – Apropos your comment of 23 January that trainspotting is 'sad', I wanted you to know that in my experience, a large number of the clergy tend to be interested in locomotives, trains and railways. Archbishop William Temple, when Headmaster of Repton, would often punish erring boys by making them work out the quickest and shortest railway routes between two parts of Britain, using Bradshaw's railway guide.
Revd Clifford Warren, Cardiff

He's jolly lucky he didn't do it in this day and age, with our sensitivity to child abuse. He'd probably get several consecutive life sentences – and quite right too, in my opinion.

But the fact that the clergy engage in a particular practice does not automatically make it cool. I know clergy who brew beer, collect stamps, and even one who is a member of the British Society for Miniature Water Lily Enthusiasts. (And he's not particularly small.) Now that is positively tragic.

DEAR ANNE – Could it be that 'uncool' clergy hobbies – defined by you on 6 February as home-brewing and a passion for water lilies – are not 'sad' if they stop us taking ourselves too seriously?
Revd Peter Canning, Nuneaton

DEAR ANNE – As the only clergyman who belongs to the International Water Lily Society, I can only imagine that your column was referring to me. I am mortified to learn that my case is 'positively tragic'.

Please will you help me drown my sorrows by sending me a bottle of that famous Atkins home-brew, which I remember so well from our student days?
Revd Charles Overton, High Wycombe

This was below the belt: how could an old friend (at theological college with my husband) show me up in this way? Especially as my home-brew was absolutely poisonous. Still, he asked for it; what could I say, but:

Bottle on its way, Charles.

The fact that a hobby is considered utterly nerdish is an excellent reason for pursuing it. The clergy, in particular, should be making loud statements about their contempt for image.

I myself have engaged not only in home-brewing (I confess: a fair cop) but also portraiture, carpentry and now, with one of my children, I even keep bees.

Now, is there anything sadder than that?

Finally (oh how the clergy suffer):

DEAR ANNE – We live next door to our curate. My sister and I like to sunbathe in the garden. Recently, a mutual friend told us that he finds this really distracting, because his study overlooks us and he can't concentrate on writing his sermons. But we love lying in the sun, and don't want to stop. What is the Christian thing to do?
Misses S. and J., Manchester

Turn the other cheek.

11. Dead People Can't Get Parking Tickets

Inevitably, death causes agony.

When Diana, Princess of Wales died the nation almost came to a standstill. The outpouring of grief mystified the commentators, and most concluded that it was the effect of crowd hypnosis: it had simply become the fashion to weep.

This doesn't satisfactorily explain, to me, my own reaction. Never before have I mourned someone I didn't know (and certainly didn't uncritically admire). The day she died I kept the television on all day (something I never do) and kept watching footage of her. As soon as I was free that Sunday evening, I went into the garden (without telling anyone, because I was embarrassed by my own sentiments) picked a bunch of flowers, and bicycled into the gloaming, my humble little posy in my basket and a lump in my throat, to Buckingham Palace.

It wasn't until I got there that I realized how many others were doing the same.

DEAR ANNE – I was disgusted by Earl Spencer's speech at the funeral of Diana, Princess of Wales. Surely it was inappropriate to be so bitter in a place of worship, and to use a sermon to voice complaints. Shouldn't he have been trying to heal wounds rather than opening them up?
Name withheld

Well, I must confess that when I first heard his tribute, I was appalled. I wondered how his friends could have allowed someone so recently and shockingly bereaved, and so numb with rage, to speak in rawness and anger at such a public event. It occurred to me that it might have been more fitting for the Princess's family to have asked a detached member of the clergy to speak about the deceased instead – as is common at many funerals.

But then I realized how anodyne that would have been. There have been churchmen near the throne who have been brave and outspoken in the past: Thomas à Becket, Thomas More and Thomas Cranmer, for instance, who all lost their lives to monarchs they had displeased. But nowadays, there are precious few members of the Church hierarchy who would even forgo a sympathetic mention in the press or tea at Downing Street in order to spell out a few home truths. So it is unlikely that any of them would have given such a heartfelt address.

As the applause of the crowd revealed, Lord Spencer's speech touched a chord. Although many have attributed the popular appeal of what he said to his well-founded attack on the gutter press – and his veiled criticism of the

Royal Family (in my view, much better left unsaid) – I believe the reason we all responded so strongly to his tribute was much more profound.

Diana's brother was deeply affecting because he voiced the anger we all feel when someone dies. Death is so wicked, such a denial of God's original purpose and of the beauty and energy of the person He created, that we feel angry. And so we should. God's intention was, and still is, that we should live for ever. Anything less is monstrous. So in one sense, Lord Spencer was right to be angry. His strength of feeling was justified. Diana should not have died. Nor should anyone. Children should not have to grow up without their mothers. Death is an outrage. We should not go gentle into that good night; we should indeed rage against the dying of the light.

Part of the significance of her death, as I said in reply to another letter in a later chapter, was surely that it prompted the fury we all feel – and in some ways should feel – in the face of death. But maturity means learning to direct the anger at the right target.

DEAR ANNE – You implied last week that it is possible to feel angry with God. Personally, I am so angry that I have become a complete non-believer. As a terminally ill mother, I consider the fact that God is to take me away from my children – when they still need me so much – absolutely irreconcilable with a loving God. The thought of never seeing how they 'turn out' is bad enough, but I feel the loss for them even more keenly. My anger with God was initiated by the total lack of understanding and support I received from some of those upon whom I should have been able to rely – many of them churchgoers.
A mother

I sympathize. Two weeks ago, I mentioned an ill friend with young children. The fuss about the funeral of Diana, Princess of Wales didn't make it any easier for her. She died two days later. I can't remember when I have felt so angry. Not because the streets were heaped with flowers for one young mother, but because there weren't another million flowers piled at my friend's door. I was angry with everyone, quite unreasonably. With other guests at the funeral (presumably as upset as I was) for politely drinking her husband's champagne afterwards as if nothing had happened; with the organist (a dear friend) for playing quietly and slowly instead of thundering out the chords to match my rage; with the sun for shining cheerfully, and most of all – oh, yes, particularly – with God.

After I'd finished ranting at God, I started on my husband. Like God, he offered me no cosy answers. So I have no answers either.

Except this. I implore you not to turn your back on God. Any solution is only to be found in Him. If you really didn't believe, you wouldn't be angry with Him or blame Him for your mortality. And He has promised you life everlasting – so you will see your children again – if you put your trust in Him. Are you really going to let a few unsympathetic churchgoers rob your children of their faith? Don't leave them with a legacy of bitterness and spiritual loneliness. Entrust them to One who loves them even more than you do. Entrust yourself to Him, too. It is your only hope, as it is mine.

DEAR ANNE – We are a Christian family and my children know that God is all-forgiving, but that His forgiveness is dependent on repentance and belief in Jesus Christ. The grandfather of my eight-year-old's school friend has just died. He was well known in the village as a foul-mouthed, drunken bully. His wife had a miserable life, his children referred to him in the most unloving terms, and his grandchildren were afraid of him. Our vicar found that, before the man died, he had no glimmer of faith. My daughter's friend has been told that her 'granddad has gone to be with Jesus'. This has confused my children considerably. How would you explain this to them?
P.W., Somerset

Perhaps he *has* gone to be with Jesus. When we face God on the Day of Judgment, it won't much matter whether we were foul-mouthed drunken bullies or saintly nuns, since none of us has lived up to God's standards. This is why Jesus died for us, to take the punishment we all deserve. If we repent and believe in Him as our Saviour, we can be forgiven and have eternal life. But if we reject Him, we must ask ourselves: 'How shall we escape if we neglect such a great salvation?' (Hebrews 2:3). Presumably this was why Jesus spent so much of His time on earth with all the people everyone else disapproved of, because they were more likely to recognize their need for forgiveness.

However, if your vicar was right, that he had no glimmer of faith, then he rejected Jesus as surely as many sober, kind, clean-living people have before him and will after him. In which case I hope, for his sake, he hasn't gone to be with Jesus. If you had consistently turned your back on Him all your life, would you want to see the God of the universe? I can't imagine anything worse. Political correctness has so seeped into the nation's preaching that although we often hear that God is loving and merciful (which is true), we are seldom reminded that He can also be terrible.

So I suggest you tell your children that God can – and often does – forgive the worst of sinners. Tell them, too, that no one can judge another man's standing before God. But also tell them that, for someone who knowingly rejects Jesus all his life, there could be no more dreadful place to be than in His presence.

DEAR ANNE – My husband and I have recently heard that the wife of a friend of ours has terminal cancer. We have only met this lady on two or three occasions, but we liked her and feel we should make contact before she dies. But knowing what to say and how to put it into words is so difficult. Can you offer any advice?
S.A., Reading

Anything you say will feel inadequate but, over and over again, people in difficult circumstances have told me that it wasn't what people said, but the fact that they were willing to try which made the difference. What hurts is when – through embarrassment, ignorance or cowardice – friends say nothing or, worst of all, avoid the bereaved or the sick because they don't know how to comfort them. It sounds stupid, but you can start by saying, 'We don't know what to say ...' Anything that shows you care is valuable. A present, a plant or some flowers may seem feeble compared with their grief (and is), but will still be appreciated. Try to

think of something practical you could do; take round a casserole. Tell them to contact you if they need anything, but bear in mind that it's much better if you take the initiative, as they are unlikely to take you up on this.

Whatever you do, do something, however clumsy.

DEAR ANNE – With reference to your advice ('whatever you do, do something'), years ago we lived on a big RAF station full of young marrieds, babies all around us. I was sterile and we hadn't yet adopted. A young mum, whom I knew slightly, had a severely handicapped baby who died after three weeks. When I bumped into her soon afterwards, I gulped and said, 'I'm so sorry about your baby', and she talked for an hour. Years later, I was told she had said: 'No one could bear to speak to me except G.M., who had no children.'

Often, we hesitate because we think, 'It could be me, my child, my husband,' and try to avert our tragedy by ignoring another's. I always say something, however clumsy or tactless, to acknowledge the sorrow.
G.M., Aberdeen

DEAR ANNE – I am in a lot of pain and have been for much of my life. I always believed abortion was wrong, but I had my first termination when I was 19, another at 21 and my last when I was 36. I do not understand why I came to murder three of my children. It is even harder to believe God can ever forgive me. I have always believed in God, and was baptized 11 years ago, but I now feel that if I had been closer to Him, I would not have done such dreadful things. Now, I feel I cannot accept forgiveness from anyone, least of all God. I am a single mother, and have four other children, aged one to thirteen, but I feel guilty for enjoying myself with them. Sometimes, I take out my anger and shame on them. I have heard of a film called The Silent Scream. Do you know where I can get hold of it? If I had seen it when I was younger, I would not have killed my first baby, Lucy. She would have been 21 now and I would have loved her so much, and she me. So much love lost.
Name and address supplied

The film you mention, *The Silent Scream* – a powerful and moving documentary showing an abortion seen on an ultrasound scan – is obtainable for £12.95 + £1 p&p from the Society for the Protection of the Unborn Child 020 7222 5845 (information@spuc.org.uk).

But you don't need a film: you need to deal with your guilt and find forgiveness – both for your own sake and for the sake of your other children. Those, like you, who are most aware of their sins and failings are those who are closest to God. Jesus criticized the self-righteous far more than those who knew they were sinners. The last thing I want is to make you feel even more guilty; but by refusing God's forgiveness you are committing a worse sin than the one that makes you ashamed. In effect, you are telling Him that His Son's suffering wasn't enough, and that His love isn't big enough to encompass what you have done. Dare I say, it is almost arrogant to think you are so bad that God can't love you.

He doesn't have any difficulty forgiving you: He has said so. What is far harder is for you to forgive yourself. Every Christian service starts with an acknowledgment of our failings. Christianity is not for those who've got it right (and it is the nature of humanity that we never do), but for those of us who have made mistakes, and messed up our lives and those of other people. It is for people who need forgiveness: for you and me. As Jesus said, people who are healthy don't need doctors, and people who are good don't need God. He came for the rest of us.

There is only one thing you can do, but it is the most powerful thing in the world. You can pray, every day, for the grace to accept God's love. I understand you are grieving for your lost children, and you probably always will. But don't spoil your love and joy for the four lovely children you have, by punishing yourself for the three you have lost. Jesus has taken the punishment already.

DEAR ANNE – The letter from the woman who had had three abortions brought tears to my eyes. Though I now have two beautiful sons, my first child was aborted without my knowledge, let alone consent. The fact that your correspondent named her baby suggests that her first abortion was not her own choice. Perhaps she needs to pray for forgiveness for the other people involved?
A father

Thank you – and all the other readers who sent letters on this subject. Among the excellent suggestions for her were: ask a priest, perhaps a woman, to hear her confession; contact the Life Pregnancy Hotline (01926 311511) which will supply a sympathetic local counsellor; ask the Society for the Protection of the Unborn Child (020 7222 5845) to put her in touch with the British Victims of Abortion, where she will find others who have suffered similar traumas. Tragically, of course, the most vulnerable victims of abortion are beyond our help.

DEAR ANNE – I read recently in your column about a lady who had three abortions and is struggling to find forgiveness. I felt prompted to write and tell you about the Firgrove, a pregnancy counselling centre that offers free pregnancy tests, advice, information and an opportunity to explore all the options, as well as post-abortion counselling. For us, abortion is not only about the deaths of children, but also the damage being done to women.

We are all Christians, but ours is not an overtly Christian centre and there is no pressure to accept a Christian viewpoint.
Caroline Kennedy, Firgrove Pregnancy Crisis and Post-Abortion Centre 02380 783134 (Also try CAREconfidential, 0800 028 2228 www.pregnancy.org.uk)

DEAR ANNE – Can you help me? I don't get angry when I know I should. My parents died last year, but much as I loved and miss them, I can't make myself angry. I find myself thinking that death might even be good, because otherwise the old would never make way for the young. This makes me feel most unnatural, like Huckleberry Finn, who knew the right thing to do but couldn't help doing wrong. Please help me. I'm in agony.
D.R.M., Northumberland

There is nothing unnatural about your response: there is no right way to grieve – the only right way is the way that comes naturally to you. You are fortunate in being able to see the good side of your loss.

The reason you are 'in agony' is probably because you believe you are not matching up to the way other people expect you to mourn, and it may be that this makes you feel guilt. But there is nothing to feel guilty about. Other people's expectations don't matter. Your feelings are fine.

DEAR ANNE – Since I am an atheist, I don't believe in an after life – although I realize that when I die, there will have to be some sort of gathering for my family and friends. Unfortunately, I have just made my wife very unhappy by declaring that I want to be neither buried nor cremated, but plan to give my body to medical research.

Have you any suggestions about how this can take place without hurting anyone?
Name and address supplied

I suggest you contact the National Transplant Information Service (0845 60606 4000 or 0117 975 7575), and ask whether it would be possible for your wife to make contact with someone whose life has been saved, or enhanced, thanks to an organ donation. Or she could look at the case studies on their website, www.uktranspant.org.uk in the newsroom section, under 'Life Stories'. If she realized the good that organ donations can do she might change her mind and become very positive about the idea. But if she doesn't, you must change your will.

It is noble and generous to want to be useful after your death, but not at the expense of your wife's feelings. You owe your wife far more than you do a stranger, and should arrange for your body to be disposed of in a way that will best help her grieve.

DEAR ANNE – It is more than six months since my husband died, but I am tormented by thoughts that he was alone in hospital when it happened, a place he hated. I visited every day, from morning until the last bus home. But one day, I received a call at 6.30 a.m. to say he had died. I should have been there. He was the best husband to me, and I let him down. Will I ever get this out of my head? Please withhold my name, as my relatives think I have adjusted well.

Please tell your friends and relatives what you have told me. Talking about it will ease your pain. No one can say whether your husband knew he was alone at the last – but if he did, he must also have been aware that his final weeks were spent with you; he knew how much you loved him. What is certain is that it is you, not he, who is suffering now. Of course, you can't help feeling sorrow; you missed the chance to say goodbye. But you mustn't feel guilty about this; you didn't mean to let him die alone. You now owe it to him to look after yourself, and that means being open with those who love you.

DEAR ANNE – Please would you pass my comments on to the lady who wasn't with her husband when he died. We all feel guilty when we're left behind: but he knew she loved him, and wanted to be there.
Mary, Chiltington

I wish I could. A number of you have sent reassuring, comforting letters for me to forward to her. But, alas, she never sent me her address.

DEAR ANNE – You recently mentioned writing 'deceased' over one's address on junk mail before returning to sender (24 March). It sounds like a good wheeze, but it can have dire consequences. My son and his wife did this, but when they came to move house, the mortgage company insisted my daughter-in-law no longer existed. They could not be persuaded that she was anything other than dead.
Wendy Charles-Warner,
Westbury

Look on the bright side: from now on, traffic wardens will hold no fear for her. The dead can't get parking tickets.

Things to do when you're dead!

12. Nothing Under the Cassock

Questions of fashion or beauty tended to be rather more 'perplexed' than 'agonized' (which is just as well for our faith in human priorities)…

DEAR ANNE – I have recently turned 50 and I feel every year of it. My job is high profile and I meet and entertain many people. To put it bluntly, I do not always feel confident about my looks and am considering a face-lift. I have several misgivings about it, however. First, I am ashamed of my vanity. Cosmetic surgery is greeted with derision in serious circles and considered trivial when compared with other more vital life-saving surgery. I cannot take months off work so I would have to admit to my face-lift. What's the best policy? I don't feel my friends would understand.
E.L., Stow-on-the-Wold, Glos

All women considering face-lifts feel the same. Do you think all those 50-year-old stars who look 32 and swear it's because of carrot juice are doing it all with positive lifeforces and 'youth retaining genes'? If they don't tell, why should you? You would need only three weeks off work. If colleagues think you are on holiday, they will expect you to return looking good. You say you feel guilty spending money on something so vain. But it's not much more vain than going to a gym. If you didn't spend the money on cosmetic surgery, would you really spend it on someone else's life-saving surgery? I suggest you budget for double what your operation will cost you. There is an excellent charity called RAFT (Restoration of Appearance and Function Trust, 01923 835815 www.raft.ac.uk) for people who need plastic surgery – burns victims, children with cleft palates, and so on. Donate as much as you spend on yourself, and your face-lift might save a limb, even a life.

I also wanted to tell this correspondent about non-surgical face-lift exercises, for instance Eva Fraser's Facial Workout in Kensington, but there wasn't space so the reference was cut at the editorial stage (this question was in the very first column, when I was not quite accustomed to sorting someone's entire life in 2¹/₂ inches). So I felt this answer was not quite adequate.

However, I then gave an answer that was just plain wrong:

DEAR ANNE – I have really thick, frizzy hair – similar to Tina Turner's, but longer – and I am only 12 years old. Although I desperately want to straighten it, my mum and dad won't let me because they say I should be proud of my hair. But it's hard to comb, wash and tie back and, even when I do, it all sticks up and people think it hasn't been brushed. I hate it.
Name and address supplied

My hair caused me similar problems at your age. I hated my curls, loathed washing them and was immensely irritated by a family friend who called me the 'fluffy chick'. And whenever I came down for a meal having just brushed it, my mother invariably said: 'Darling, you look lovely, but I do wish you'd brush your hair.' I longed to shave it off. One day, you will probably be proud of your hair and even learn to love it. But this will happen sooner if you are allowed to do what you want with it now.

Our 12-year-old had fabulously long, blonde hair which was adored by the fathers of all her friends. But she hated it because she had to brush it all the time, so she chopped it all off one hot summer's day and had a short back and sides for two years. Luckily, she's got that phase out of her system now, and her hair has grown so much she nearly looks human again.

Ask your parents to let you have a smart, short haircut. Tell them you would find it easier to look neat if your hair was cut, and that you just want to try it in a different style for a while. After all, you can always grow it again. I hope they let you. (If not, my 14-year-old says you should brush your hair hard while blow drying – this may not be good for it, but she says it straightens the curls.)

Well, several women with Tina Turner hair wrote to me and said cutting was the worst thing to do with it …

DEAR ANNE – With reference to your 12-year-old reader with frizzy hair last week, I, too, was teased in the playground about my Brillo pad. I was saved by John Frieda's Frizz-Ease hair serum. Also, hair straighteners make the mess manageable and VO5 hot-oil treatments are great for shine. I desperately want your correspondent to try these before she cuts her hair, because curls take so long to grow again.
Miss Tanya Salminen, London W1

DEAR ANNE – My solutions for frizz: keep hair long because the weight keeps the curls down, use a conditioner, never towel-dry, comb through with a wide-toothed comb and set with gel... and marry a man with blond hair: I now have three flaxen-haired children.
Karen Davis, Angus, Tayside

PS. Your column infuriates me, but I find your principles, and the fact that you publish letters that are critical of you, refreshing.

I still thought they should let the poor girl cut her hair if she wanted to.

Sometimes I had to read a letter over and over again, convinced that I had somehow missed the point:

DEAR ANNE – I was preparing to go to a party with my wife of 25 years, when she announced that she had a surprise for me. When I turned round to look, she was dressed as a man: in a jacket and trousers, one of my shirts, a tie and a waistcoat. I was shocked and said I would not go out with her looking like that; after all, how would she feel if I dressed as a woman?
R.P., Northallerton

I have to confess to being stumped by your question. I often wear a jacket and trousers, frequently pinch my husband's shirts and have been known to creep out of the house in a rather fanciable silk jacket that I gave him. But I'm pleased to say that the only time he wears a miniskirt is to do his Andrews Sisters routine at the church panto. And I would be jolly fed up if he wore stilettos or make-up as a matter of course.

This is not as inconsistent as it sounds. It is socially acceptable for women to wear trousers, and we look feminine in them. But transvestites are trying to imitate members of the opposite sex or be mistaken for them, which is rather different. It sounds to me as if your wife was just trying to be inventive and fashionable. She was probably disappointed that you did not like her new style. If, however, she is genuinely trying to look like a man, that is a rather different matter, and I suggest that you write to me again.

On the Radio 4 programme Any Questions, there is usually time for a question at the end that is quick, witty and unpredictable: for this reason modern politicians often dread it, because their extensive research team has not been able to put in a week's work preparing the correct answer for them. But for an ignorant idiot like me, who has spent the rest of the programme in sheer terrified panic in case a question is sprung on me about some world leader I've never heard of, this is the moment to savour: my ordeal is nearly over, soon I will be having a delicious dinner with really interesting people (TV techies are great fun) and this question is unlikely to make more of a fool of me than anyone else.

From the very first week of my column, I realized I liked these kind of questions more than any other, and always tried to include at least one each week, at the end:

DEAR ANNE – My face in repose looks naturally grumpy, even when I am content. Short of having plastic surgery, how can I stop people telling me to 'cheer up love, it may never happen'?
G.A., Sheffield

Wear a T-shirt saying 'I've cheered up now, so LEAVE ME ALONE.'

"I said, I've cheered up!"

DEAR ANNE – I am not sure whether to continue to wear the Marks & Spencer tie that I bought for my wedding 15 years ago. I fear it makes me: a) untrendy; b) a fashion victim; c) a replica of my father; or d) just rather sad. What do you think?
Keith Rylands, Maidstone

I think you are: a) too well-dressed to bother about fashion; b) too macho to have problems with image; c) too busy to shop; or d) too contented to care.

Wear the tie or frame it, but don't throw it away.

I do sometimes wonder why I bother:

> **After your advice not to dispose of my tie, I retained it for years but eventually pressure on my tie rack became overwhelming ...**
> **Keith Rylands**

Despite his attempt to disguise it, he had obviously taken no notice of my advice at all. And I had given it so much thought ...

DEAR ANNE – I am severely overweight, and beginning to dread the stares on the beach. Any ideas?
R.J., Middlesex

Get a friend to photograph you, just as you are, in your skimpiest and least flattering bikini. Stick the photo on your fridge for all (particularly you yourself) to see. It won't help you in time for this year, but you should look great by next.

DEAR ANNE – I am a single woman living in a two-bedroom flat. I recently agreed to let a friend of a friend stay for a month, until the house he is buying becomes available. He is very nice, but has a rather disconcerting habit of wandering about in his Y-fronts. When he chats to me in the kitchen, I find it impossible to eat my breakfast. What should I do?
D.T., London NW6

Tell him to take them off. Boxer shorts, perhaps; Y-fronts, never.

DEAR ANNE – I am confused. I always thought we should try not to be provocative in our attire, and now Germaine Greer is telling us all to throw away our undies. What's a good feminist to do?
Jane Copeland (Ms),
London SW7

I am rather old-fashioned about this. Knickers are a thoroughly modern invention, and I can't see any point in them at all.

DEAR ANNE – Your recent column (19 May) went over the top. Go without knickers indeed! And from a vicar's wife.

I am disgusted. Are men to go without trousers?
Miss M.S., Worthing

Good idea. Real men wear nothing under their kilts – or cassocks.

13. Will We Ever See Our Son Again?

Sometimes, readers wrote to me simply wanting information: I spent quite a lot of time on the telephone, just finding things out. Occasionally they needed practical, prosaic help: one correspondent couldn't get her dustbin emptied because her neighbour had put cat litter in it, so I rang her council who cleared it out the next day.

If the question demanded more specialist knowledge, I would shamelessly exploit a wide network of long-suffering friends in various professions. I have a wonderful girlfriend of many years' standing, a GP with a superbly robust attitude to every kind of ailment, who should undoubtedly have been paid a commission for all the times I rang her up to demand the medical answer to stress-induced post-natal earache. (Her advice to every illness is refreshingly the same. She claims to have modelled her bedside manner on my sympathetic parenting, and treats her patients as I treat my children. 'Doctor, I have terrible pains in my back, legs, chest, head ...' 'Oh dear, what a shame,' she says kindly. *Next!*')

Usually, my friends' expert advice made perfect sense and I would relay it back to the reader with great confidence. However, there was one occasion when I passed on the professional comments of an extremely experienced and knowledgeable friend, rather against my better judgment – and very much lived to regret it.

This was the letter that sparked it all off:

DEAR ANNE – While our son was at university, he had a crisis. He felt constantly stressed and then became unable to cope with life as he had before. Finally, he sought help from a counsellor whom he has seen regularly ever since. He is now 30. Last year, he said he wanted to distance himself from us and, for 12 months, we haven't seen him. Our only contact has been three phone calls and cards on our birthdays. We have always been supportive and find all this a mystery. Is there any name for this syndrome, or a support group or special advice for parents in our position? We think that we may not see him again.
Name and address supplied

I found this story rather alarming, but when I rang – among others – a psychiatrist whom I know well and respect greatly, he reassured me that the counselling must have been necessary and would do good in the long run, so this is what I replied:

I have discussed the case with professionals in different fields (including counselling and psychiatry), and they are not aware of a name for this, or a support group. Bear in mind that your son had problems before he asked for help, and try to accept that the counsellor may be giving him what he needs. Possibly, by being very loving, caring parents, you tried almost too hard and became too involved. Every child has to become independent eventually, and those who are very close to their families sometimes have to make the break more abruptly than others.

Try also to consider any mistakes you may have made when he was growing up. Perhaps you could write and tell him where you think you went wrong, and ask him what he thinks. You could also ask his forgiveness. If your relationship with your son was basically good, it will almost certainly recover over time. The best thing you can do is to keep giving him support when he asks for it. Maintain contact. Treat him as a fellow adult. And don't give up.

What I was soon to discover, from the influx of similar letters that this one prompted, was that there certainly should be a name for this syndrome, that it was alarming that the counselling and psychiatric professionals knew nothing of it, and that there would eventually be a tiny and informal support group – if only of my correspondents.

In future, I replied from my own experience, though I still seemed to feel obliged to defend counselling:

DEAR ANNE – Our daughter, now in her late twenties, found herself single, unemployed and lacking direction, so she sought help from a counsellor. After a few weeks of treatment, she said she needed space to sort herself out and refused to have any more to do with us.

Naturally, we were devastated. My husband and I both wrote to her, apologizing for any mistakes we might have made in her upbringing. We never received a reply. Whenever we telephoned, her answerphone was on and she never returned our calls. Last autumn, she moved house and didn't give us her new address. We haven't spoken to her for more than a year.

We love our daughter very much, and feel absolutely bereaved. We are convinced that her counsellor poisoned her against us – perhaps with 'false memory syndrome'. Please, can you offer us any hope?
Name and address supplied

Your situation is not uncommon. I have received similar letters from parents who feel they have lost their children through counselling. 'False memory' can be very dangerous. However, counselling should not be dismissed altogether: some is excellent and very helpful.

The Salvation Army Family Tracing Service* can help you track down immediate members of your family, and will forward post if your daughter doesn't want you to know where she lives. But the real issue is her reluctance to talk to you. The best advice I can give you is simply to hang on. Drop her a line from time to time, keeping her abreast of family news. Don't ask for a reply, or expect one.

Parenting can sometimes be a costly, one-way business: you didn't expect her to thank you when she was in nappies and you may need to adopt the same attitude now.

If there are other family members to whom she will talk, you could use them as intermediaries and sources of information.

Just be there. One day, with luck, she will return.

*(www2.salvationarmy.org.uk)

But the letters continued to come:

DEAR ANNE – I am convinced that my problem with my 29-year-old daughter is connected with the counselling she was given. I think our modern, affluent society seems riddled with 'false counselling syndrome'.
P.G., Wells

I have had many letters on this subject, and not one saying a counsellor has been any help. Certainly the only psychologist who ever helped us, as a family, did so by doing something practical: finding a place for one of our children at a Special Needs school.

If you are having counselling, you should always avoid like the plague anyone who tries to cut you off from your family or the people you love. Other danger signs are being deprived of sleep or basic nutrients or being swamped with suffocating love: these are all established brain-washing techniques.

The original letter I received was from a woman whose grown-up son had chosen to be counselled. In this instance, the best policy is usually to assume the best and be supportive. If you say you think your child's counsellor is a dangerous control-freak, you are likely to make a strained relationship worse. However, if you are close to your child, there are times when questioning the counsellor's wisdom can work.

The best defences against an adult son or daughter becoming involved with a bad counsellor are laid in early childhood. I believe a child should know there is nothing he can say or do, however wicked, to put himself beyond his parents' love.

DEAR ANNE – Your column last week, in which a correspondent wrote about losing a daughter through therapy, gave me my best night's sleep for almost a year. My daughter is a professional of 35, with two beautiful children, a loving husband and secure finances. After therapy, she refused to speak to me, left the answerphone on and never returned calls. My heart is broken. I live alone and didn't want to confide in friends, as I assumed it must be my fault – though I don't know what I have done wrong. I had believed myself to be the only one on earth with this heartache.
M.A., Beccles

I have had numerous letters saying the same thing. It may not be your fault at all. Presumably, your daughter has lost her father (through separation or death), and it wouldn't be uncommon for her to take her feelings about this out on you. I suggest you let her (or perhaps her husband) know how much you miss her. Do try to share your worries with a friend. It must be awful to go through this by yourself.

What was striking was the remarkable similarity of the stories: a previously happy family with loving parents; one of the offspring just entering adulthood; the initial problem relatively minor; counselling sought for something that would almost certainly have sorted itself out without the family subsequently broken up and destroyed; the parents heartbroken as well as utterly mystified.

At the time I had a wonderful secretary, Jenny, who dealt with my letters for one afternoon a week. (I don't have her any more, so please be patient if you should ever write to me; it sometimes takes me two or three years to get to the bottom of my in-tray.) I asked her to contact all those who had written to me on the subject, asking whether they would like their details circulated; having done so, she then put them in touch with each other. It was a small gesture, and I have no idea whether it was any help or encouragement, but I thought it was the least I could do.

There had to be another side to the story:

DEAR ANNE – My father showed me the letter from the mother who has lost contact with her daughter after counselling (21 May). I'm so grateful. I am 31, an only child, happily married, pregnant, successful and close to my dad. But, for various reasons, I have felt the need for counselling.

My therapist hasn't told me what to do, but showed me that I needn't always be subject to my mother's control, which I have

come to see as evil. When I described some past incidents to my mother, she dismissed them as products of a 'false memory'. Since I broke contact with her, my life has improved beyond my wildest dreams.
T.C., Kent

Your letter upset me profoundly, because I have received so many letters from heartbroken parents who believe that counsellors have taken away their children. The fact that you feel good doesn't mean anything. All sorts of destructive things feel great at first – heroin, gambling, adultery – otherwise nobody would bother with them.

Whatever you blame your mother for, you must surely recognize that she must now be devastated. Real maturity involves relating to people properly, not avoiding them. Please make contact with her as soon as you can.

I can't help wondering what motive your father had in showing you the article. More to the point, what kind of therapist would prompt her client to see her own mother as evil?

Of course, not all 'counselling' is the same. Ringing the Samaritans, or sitting in the vicar's kitchen with a cup of tea, is obviously unlikely to do anyone any harm. And Cognitive Behavioural Therapy is a defined programme of treatment with proven beneficial effects. By contrast it is that form of counselling loosely called psychotherapy that can be so destructive. And in the years since, I have become more and more dismayed at the tragic effect that psychotherapeutic counselling can have upon previously happy families.

Despite everything I had learnt from this episode, when our own daughter became ill I told myself I must remain open-minded, and paid for her to see a psychotherapist. He did her untold damage, hurt her dreadfully, and eventually behaved with shocking disregard for her feelings, her future or her familial relationships.

Now I know more about psychotherapy, both at a personal and at an academic level, than I did when that first letter arrived. And once or twice since, I have publicly voiced my reservations about it. Whenever I do, a few more people write to me with the same heartbroken tale:

DEAR ANNE – We also think we may never see our son again. He is 35 and last saw us in 1995. Like the son of your correspondent, he has distanced himself – on the advice of his counsellor – and we haven't even received birthday cards. We feel helpless. Thankfully, we have two other sons who are fine.
Mrs P.C., Leicester

I also became more aware of research that suggests we should use old-fashioned self-control, rather than indulge in a so-called therapeutic expression of every negative feeling:

DEAR ANNE – Two years ago, after a redundancy forced me to travel 300 miles a day to work, one of my closest male friends started spending a lot of time with my wife. One day, I came home early and saw the pair of them on the sofa, half-undressed. I hoped the affair would run its course, but my wife became obsessed with my friend and eventually left me and our seven-year-old son to be with him. I lost my job because of the strain. He has now finished with her, having had his bit of fun (as he has with other women before), with no loss of position (as a magistrate), or respect, money, or his marriage. I have lost everything: my wife, my job, soon my home and any financial security for my old age and my son's education. My only consolation is that I still have my son's love and company. I know revenge is a base and unworthy desire, but I want to see this man lose as much as I have. These feelings are damaging to myself and my family but they are very strong. How can I be rid of them? T.W., Nottinghamshire

A study showed recently that, contrary to all expectation, a British stiff upper lip gets its bearer through bereavement quicker than indulging in grief and self-pity. Unfortunately, it's become unfashionable to suppress our feelings, so we don't get much practice or encouragement. But it is a necessary social skill – and essential in your situation. Find safe ways of venting your emotions.

Your GP can arrange for you to see a counsellor, who is paid to listen to your anger. It can sometimes help to write a scathing letter to someone who's wronged you, explaining your viewpoint; then hide it in a drawer and eventually, when it has served its pur-pose, throw it away. Buy yourself a punchball or gym membership or, best of all, learn a new sport – with your son: physical exercise channels aggression very constructively.

Learn from other people's mistakes. Compare those in the news who say they live for revenge (sometimes 30 years after they lost their children) with Gordon Wilson, whose daughter was killed at Enniskillen and who remembered her in his peace efforts: I know whom I'd rather be like.

If you enjoy the theatre, many Elizabethan 'revenge' plays, such as Kyd's *The Spanish Tragedy* or Shakespeare's *Titus Andronicus*, show how lives are ruined by the thirst for revenge. If you are a believer, remind yourself that vengeance belongs to the Lord. And most of all, be ruthlessly objective. You have not lost everything. You have your son. He, not your 'friend', deserves your time and energy. Don't allow the man who took his mother away to steal his father, too.

DEAR ANNE – I am sorry that you preceded your worthwhile suggestions to Mr T.W. last week with an assertion that he should suppress his feelings. This is not to be recommended as it increases the risk of personality deterioration, stress-related disease, and mental breakdown. Suppression? No. Expression? An emphatic yes. J.D.C., London

Mr T.W. told me that his desire for revenge was damaging him and his family and asked how to overcome it. My dictionary defines 'suppress' as: 'to put an end to, prohibit, hold in check, restrain … to exercise self control'.

I can't speak for you, but I have to suppress numerous feelings every day: overwhelming desires to bawl at the children, hurl my computer out of the window, disagree with my neighbours and run my handlebars along the gleaming Mercedes which has just edged my bicycle into the gutter. I don't know (or much care) whether this suppression is causing irreparable damage to my personality, but it certainly helps form my character. After all, my family would suffer

rapid deterioration (and possibly depletion) if I didn't exercise a bit of suppression.

Clearly, if we are unsuccessful in suppressing destructive feelings and merely rearrange them, we haven't solved the problem. Anger, directed inwards, can make us depressed and even accident-prone.

Mr T.W.'s rage is understandably strong, so I suggested various remedies to help him to conquer – or suppress – it. It's high time we were liberated from this post-Sixties, oppressive tyranny of our feelings. Some feelings are wonderful. Others are awful. Being an adult human means exercising control. Mental breakdown: no. Mature and civilized control? Very much so.

DEAR ANNE – Thank you for your thought-provoking reply to my letter about revenge. The sense of betrayal and loss is difficult to deal with and my belief wavers and sometimes disappears, but I know you are right to tell me to be controlled. I have arranged to see a counsellor in early June (poor man!) and my son is, as ever, my first priority. We have a close, loving relationship and I have told him that he should direct his pain and anger at me, rather than letting it out at school, which would only hurt him. T.W., Nottinghamshire

14. A Sex-Charged Correspondence

There was one correspondent who wrote to me more than any other (eventually prompting a complaint from another reader that we were conducting an illicit epistolary liaison) who deserves a chapter all to himself. I was looking forward to editing it, and it was the first that I did.

Courtesy Noel Ford

And it immediately presented a logistical problem. It's one thing to send out a circular asking permission to republish a letter or two, offering, for the sake of mutual convenience, to take silence as consent. It's another matter altogether to dedicate an entire chapter to a former relationship, without specifically checking that there hasn't been a cooling off over the years. He was such a faithful correspondent I was convinced he would smile on my venture. But, as he once said to me, 'Who can tell?' Perhaps he had come to regard me as his ex-agony aunt, and wanted no reminder of what had once been. Perhaps he has even now formed affections for Deirdre on The Sun, or the formidable Claire Raynor, and doesn't want the embarrassment of what once passed between us.

The most straightforward thing, of course, would have been to ask him. But here the plot thickens. In between my writing letters to all those in my carefully preserved box file, and my getting down to the nitty gritty of doing the work of editing, we moved house. Plenty of people do. But – for some no doubt very good reason that momentarily escapes me – we did this in a rather novel way.

Previously, we lived in a spacious, capacious and wonderfully accommodating vicarage, containing fourteen years of our lives and loves, hopes and fears, and more to the present point, possessions. Including box files. Containing the addresses of all my correspondents. It being a working vicarage, it went with Shaun's job as vicar. What could be more natural, therefore, than for us to leave this dearly beloved place so that he could take up another job with a different church. One which had however, unfortunately, temporarily mislaid its clergy housing.

It must have seemed like a good idea at the time.

The good news is that our possessions (and box files) have been stored comfortably and securely. The bad news is that we haven't. So everything we own apart from a few clothes, my complete works of Shakespeare, Chaucer and Plato, and one or two other essentials we grabbed from the bookshelves as we fled, is now luxuriously sheltering in a Pickfords lock-up – or rather, about twenty five Pickfords lock-ups – reputedly in Ealing somewhere. Presumably you've got to use Ealing for something.

I know, I know. If I had had foresight, and planned the whole book in advance thinking of everything I might need a year ago, then as I glanced round my home for one last time to say goodbye, asking myself whether the baby needed extra cot blankets or I could survive the next year without that particular book and whether my heart would break, I would suddenly have shouted to myself, 'Box file!'. A more organised writer, dashing out of the house in the midst of fire or flood, would have thought of it. I'm sorry. We all have our little failings.

No matter. When I (skidding wildly over an already taut deadline) proudly sent this chapter as a sample of more to come (drip-feeding my publisher to maintain dependency, as it were) my editor Tony Collins (instead of drooling for more, which had been my Cunning Plan) calmly asked whether I had permission. Permission? This is my friend. We go back years. Besides, he would (along with everyone else) have been sent a letter asking for copyright a year ago, blithely telling him not to reply unless he had a problem.

Nonetheless, Tony said firmly. Possibly slightly more firmly than was strictly necessary.

Oh go on then, I said grudgingly; contact him if you really want to. This being the Age of Information, when everyone in the world can be found at the press of Google.

Yes, well. For some idiotic reason the person answering (or rather, more accurately, not answering) to his name, living in his town, had perversely decided to go ex-directory, Tony reported. So? I replied. We'll find him another way. All right, Tony said. How?

It came to me at three in the morning, as the best ideas do. Once before, I had wanted to find the name of some people who were selling a pretty house in Dorset somewhere, without bothering the poor overworked estate agent who thought they'd changed their minds about selling it, and had persuaded the kind librarian in Dorchester Library to raid the Electoral Register. My memory was that this method had been slightly dubious – I had had to do some serious sweet-talking – but it had worked before and would again. Nobody, in this brave new world of documentation and data, can hide for long.

Brighton Library couldn't give that kind of information over the telephone. Yes, I knew that: a paltry detail. What did cause me to pause, however, was that Electoral Registers are recorded, not by name, but by address. I'd momentarily forgotten this trivial annoyance. The librarian couldn't look him up, however successfully I persuaded. Not without the address. Come on, I urged reasonably; give me some help here. There was nothing I could do. Unless it was an emergency, and I went to the police.

Well, it was, obviously. As the reader will discover – the day your kitten climbs up a drainpipe and you try to wash it down with a bucket of water and you then hang out of the window drying it off with a hair dryer while your children wail until you ring the RSPCA who tell you to contact the police who suggest you ring the Fire Brigade because they're probably between fires – as any reader will discover if you have children for long enough, emergency services spend a large part of their day hanging around waiting for emergencies to happen and longing to put their emergency skills into practice.

I told the police everything – the containers in Ealing, the forgotten friendship –

and they quite adorably gave me his postcode. There you are, I said to Tony. The local post office can't fail to know him. He is that kind of person.

An address would be nice, Tony said. There's no pleasing some people. I rang the library back and said, there's this friend of mine; I've got his postcode from the police (that impressed them). Please be an absolute sweetie … I mean, if I were there in person, in the library – which I would be, if I had world enough and time.

With a flourish of triumph and a cry of Bingo, I delivered the full postal address to Tony. Of the wrong person. Who wrote back in some bemusement.

I had a vague idea that the copyright requirement, which the law in this country drearily insists upon, is that one should make 'every reasonable effort'. I might not have done it reasonably, but I had certainly made an effort. Surely, I said to Tony; haven't we?

Why not put this chapter in Volume Two, he said. When you've emptied the containers in Ealing.

It was while I was attempting to trace the Indonesian Embassy for our daughter Serena (don't ask) that I gave it one last go and asked Directory Enquiries, as I was on the telephone to them anyway. There are four people of that name, in that area, they told me. All ex-directory.

After I'd finished blasting and bothering, Serena said, darkly, that she has a friend who has some method and I absolutely wasn't to tell him she'd said so because he would never speak to her again.

Ring him immediately, I said.

I know you're never going to speak to me again, I overheard her saying, but Mummy … and here her voice became low and quiet and I couldn't catch any more. She handed the telephone to me. Name? He asked me. Town? Hair colour, mother's maiden name, unsavoury habits in bed? I didn't know him that well, I protested. He rang me back ten minutes later with three likelies and a long shot.

Don't ask any awkward questions, I said to Tony. Just write to them.

Ten days later, he forwarded to me an anxious and aggrieved letter from the daughter of an elderly gentleman. An innocent *Times* reader who had never, in all his born days, picked up a copy of *The Daily Telegraph* let alone written to its agony aunt. The threat to publicize his name had caused him great distress, probably hastened his end, and how in the name of goodness had we got his contact details? (He presumably having gone to the trouble of being ex-directory, and all.)

And? Tony asked me.

Just tell her, I said contritely, that I gave them to you.

I was bowed and almost broken. It would be good copy for the detective novel. But for the purposes of the present book, it was discouraging. The faint scream of the desperate deadline had turned to a deafening siren. So we're cutting the chapter? I said, beaten.

I think, Tony said kindly, we have made every reasonable effort. I agree he will almost certainly love it. Go ahead, publish, and pray we're not damned.

(I wanted to kiss him. And would have done, if I hadn't been so late returning the proofs.)

So here it is.

For some reason that I cannot now begin to remember or excuse, the first time I published a letter from him, I got his name wrong. (It is seared on my memory now – and on that of the combined security and library forces in the Brighton area – but it wasn't then.) His second letter was a slightly sharp note to that effect, which I kept to myself: I was too embarrassed to publicize the fact that I had made such an elementary and sloppy mistake. So the next time I answered a letter from him, I simply used his initials… little realizing that his name would soon become such an integral part of my column.

DEAR ANNE – Your advice not to post a letter but to put it in a drawer until a row has blown over is ridiculous. If we all followed your instructions, you would get precious little feedback for your column. I have had cause to write several such letters. I didn't hesitate to post them, thus avoiding mounting frustration and festering epistles nestling among my Y-fronts. It wasn't easy, but it is better to have things aired openly.
Harry Lowe, Hove

Thank you for sending me a beautiful example of a letter which would have been better left festering among garments that we now know rather more about than we necessarily wanted to … (You'll be relieved to know that my full reply is firmly buried under my stockings.)

DEAR ANNE – I am not relieved to know that your full reply to me is buried beneath your stockings. Every time you go to the drawer in search of an unsnagged pair of 15 denier Wolford seamless, you will be reminded of your letter, languishing stifled. I beseech you, post it today.
H.L., Hove

Fear not. It is summer, I am bare-legged; I will not be reminded of you for months. When I am, I shall feel smug at having refrained from the fray. But you are causing me sleepless nights. Do I look like a woman who wears 'seamless' stockings? Before I know it, someone will accuse me of owning a pair of tights.

DEAR ANNE – Your reply to my letter last week asked if you look like a woman who wears seamless hosiery. I'm afraid it's quite impossible to say: my Great Aunt Laetitia, who resembled Whistler's grandmother, was found to be wearing Janet Reger underwear when she was discovered

slumped over her petit-point. So who can tell?
Harry Lovelock, Hove

I don't for a moment believe you, but I know when I'm beaten. You win. Touchée.

I remember having a disagreement with the Features Editor, Corinna Honan, as to whether 'touchée' should have an extra e on the end. I, having done fencing as school, was convinced it should – to denote the gender of the one who had sustained the hit; Corinna, who is half French, said it should not – on the grounds that she had never, in her life, seen it spelt in such an extraordinary way. She, being the editor, naturally had her way in the *Telegraph*; I, being the author, have amended it at last. (And I'm happy to say, have continued the academic debate with Corinna, who corrects me: "Your quote isn't quite right, in that of course I've seen it spelt with two e's – as in, elle était très touchée." And then adds, very graciously. "Heck – maybe you were right after all." The search for semantic precision continues. Corinna even suggested I could look it up in a dictionary … But I thought that would really be taking the pursuit of excellence too far.)

DEAR ANNE – I am bemused, mystified and amazed at the current outpouring of national grief. Although I feel sorry for her immediate family, I never knew Diana, Princess of Wales, wasn't interested in her comings and goings and never bought a tabloid newspaper so I could ogle her kissing whomsoever. I do find the mass hysteria incomprehensible.
Harry Lovelock, Hove

Then you are unusual. Aristotle explained that tragedy should evoke both pity and terror in order to be truly cathartic. The tragic figure must be like us to inspire the terror; above us to prompt the pity; and the fall must come about through a fatal flaw in the tragic character, not because of random malice from the gods. The literary critic A.C. Bradley defined a tragedy as 'a story of exceptional calamity leading to the death of a man in high estate'.

Diana had all the classic qualities of the true tragic protagonist. Initially almost frumpy, she was like the girl next door, so we could all identify with her: unhappy children, neglected wives, mousey teenagers and bulimic girls all felt that Diana represented their troubles; the sick, the disabled and the elderly knew she loved and cared about people just like them. And yet, like a dramatic heroine, she was as far above us as the stars, with a grace that made her more regal than the Royals, a beauty that made her the most photographed woman in the world, and a glamour more startling than any Oscar winner's. And her terrible end came about entirely because of the person she was, the story driven by her own fateful character.

We all need catharsis. Diana's life and death form a tragedy, which we can identify with as we do with the story of King Lear or Antigone. And just as we need to celebrate life's joys, so we also need to mourn its sorrows. A friend of mine, a mother with sons the same age as the Princes, is dying. By mourning Diana, I am also mourning my friend and all like her. When I wept on Sunday, I wept for the sorrows we all suffer in our lives.

DEAR ANNE – In your reply to Mr Lovelock, with whom I agree, you might have found space to mention a few more people who could have identified with the late Princess: disloyal wives, manipulative divorcees, unchaste women, etc. ...
G.B. Dawe, Watford

Yes, I could have done. But it isn't always necessary to state the obvious. And I don't think my children would want to read a list of my failings just after losing me. And, living as I do in the glass house of my own sin, I try to remember what Our Lord said in a similar situation about chucking too many stones.

DEAR ANNE – I find myself in serious disagreement with one of your replies. Your correspondent last week, Harry Lovelock, is not unusual in finding the mass hysteria over the death of Diana incomprehensible.
Name and address supplied

DEAR ANNE – Mr Lovelock is not unusual.
Heather Cowan, Langshott

DEAR ANNE – I do not find Harry Lovelock unusual.
Mrs G.E. Orwin, Peterborough
PS. Karen Davis is not alone in finding your column infuriating.

Okay, okay. I've had a pile of letters telling me the same thing. He is not alone. The odd ones out were the two million on the streets of London last Saturday. And the 31 million watching at home. And the 2.5 billion tuning in across the world. And me. Mr Lovelock, who has triumphed over me in this column before, wins again.

Before this next one to me, there was a letter from Mr Harry Lovelock on the *Telegraph* editorial page. I was obviously not giving him enough to do: would my most loyal letter writer prove unfaithful? Soon, I'm happy to say, his correspondence found its natural home again.

DEAR ANNE – To get to the bottom line immediately, why, from the age of 50 or so, do men start to lose their derrières? We grow paunches, fill our waist lines, and produce mammaries a girl would swoon to emulate, but our bottoms fade away, leaving nothing but flapping trouser. As I have joined this unhappy band, I would appreciate an answer to my deep-seated problem.
Harry Lovelock, Hove

I'm afraid you have a stark choice. Either buy an electric-blue shell-suit and go running around the park, getting sweaty and embarrassing your friends, in an attempt to revamp your muscle tone. Or learn to enjoy and accept the physical symptoms of your age by smoking a pipe, investing in a good single malt whisky, stoking up a fire and sinking into a rocking chair. I strongly advise the latter. My husband has just bought a pair of half-moon spectacles that make him look twice his age. I find them absurdly attractive, and have thereby come to the conclusion that accepting one's age – or even augmenting it – is extremely sexy. I would counsel you to accept your dignified, older derrière. You could, of course, compromise by acquiring a gentlemanly dog who politely suggests a walk from time to time.

"Touché!"

DEAR ANNE – Your advice to Harry Lovelock was both superficial and dangerous. A 50-year-old man doing nothing but sitting in front of the fire, smoking and drinking whisky? How long will he last doing that? He could swim regularly or join a rambling club. If you are going to do this job (money for old rope, incidentally) then at least take it seriously.
Mr Jones, Merseyside

Mr Lovelock has written me several witty and humorous letters. In fact, his enthusiasm as a correspondent to me and others probably explains why he has a problem with his sagging derrière: he spends too long on it penning charming epistles. I have to tread a careful path: if I suggest too sedentary a life his health may deteriorate, leading him to do less writing…or even expire altogether. But if he joins a gym – or a rambling club – he will also have less time for his correspondence. And if I insult him by taking his letters too seriously, he might stop writing to me altogether. I treasure correspondents with a sense of humour because they help me cope with those critics who have none.

DEAR ANNE – For some time now, I have had a crush on a glamorous columnist who writes for a national daily. Recently, I offered her some considered advice, and she accused me of having no sense of humour!

She is conducting a sex-charged correspondence with some other fellow, and her so-called job (something of a sinecure) is obviously a front for this liaison.
Mr Jones, Merseyside

Faint heart never won a round of Bingo. Lavish her with the usual – orchids, champagne and diamonds – and before you know it, you will have driven your wretched rival out of what passes for her mind.

Valentine's Day

DEAR ANNE – Do you believe, as did Turgenev, that 'There is always one that loves and one that is loved'?
Harry Lovelock, Hove

DEAR ANNE – I am extremely worried. I have agreed with everything you have said for the past eight months.
Harry Lovelock, Hove

Indeed, I do. I agree with the Dowager Lady Byron:

> Women's love is in her life a
>   part time thing,
> 'Tis a man's whole existence.

Believe me, you're not half as worried as I am.

---

15. Gentlemen Prefer Us

It is a scientifically proven fact that blondes see the world differently.

Also Valentine's Day

DEAR ANNE – I am a good-looking blonde, employed in research. My problem is my supervisor – he makes my pulse race. How can I disclose my feelings in a gentle way? I don't want to put him off, and don't know how to approach him. Please help.
A frustrated blonde,
S.R., London

This year is not a leap year, but it's unreasonable to expect you to wait for one. So you will just have to bite the bullet. Don't hang about: ask him out tonight. If he turns you down, you will have to forget him and move on – but why would he? As an attractive blonde you will surely know how to give him a wonderful evening and make him feel terrific – without giving anything away. (Play it cool, not so much because you have to face each other on Monday morning but because it's better to play it cool.)
    Have fun. Above all, remember: Gentlemen Prefer Us.

DEAR ANNE – In your replies on St Valentine's Day, you ended one letter with the phrase: 'Gentlemen Prefer Us'. This put me in mind of a Raymond Chandler remark: 'It was a blonde. A blonde to make a bishop kick a hole in a stained glass window.' Watch out next time you and your husband get an episcopal visit!
J.A. (son of a bishop), Bridport

DEAR ANNE – Whenever we're out, my boyfriend eyes up the talent across the road and compares me (unfavourably) with the leggy blondes he sees. I'm fed up with competing. What do you suggest?
A.R., Manchester

Cross the road.

DEAR ANNE – My boyfriend and I have accepted a party invitation from a friend who owns a model agency. His house will be full of gorgeous, skinny women. How do I compete?
A.R., London

Easy. Just wait. Sooner or later, they will open their mouths and speak.

Indeed, as all true blondes know, there is – regardless of hair colour – what one might call a blonde approach to life:

DEAR ANNE – An ex-boyfriend from years back keeps treating me to expensive theatre tickets and taking me out to smart restaurants afterwards. I find it almost impossible to turn him down, because I secretly enjoy these treats. However, I don't want to give him the wrong idea. What should I do?
A.S., Stockwell

Stop being so silly: he's a grown man, and an ex-boyfriend. He won't get the wrong idea unless you give it to him, which you will only do if you insist on feeling guilty.

If he likes to pay for the pleasure of your company, let him – or give him my telephone number.

DEAR ANNE – My boyfriend is broke, but won't stop taking me out for expensive meals. How can I dissuade him?
R.A., London SW7

Don't even think of it, unless you want to marry him. Naturally, if you were struggling to meet mortgage repayments, school fees, the weekly shop and the bills for your Jimmy Choos, his extravagance would be trying. But, in the short term, he sounds just the ticket.

DEAR ANNE – A colleague keeps sending me tokens of her affection. Every time I get to my desk, I find a flower or a little sweet. I like her, but not in that way. What should I do?
John G., London

Open a flower and little sweet shop?

Seriously, send her tokens of male affection. You know: washing-up gloves, dusters, cookbooks. If that doesn't put her off, I'm afraid there's nothing else for it: you'll have to marry her.

Our son is at a slightly eccentric school that has its own language and vocabulary, going back 600 years. No one who isn't a past or present pupil can understand or converse in it.

A similar thing is true of blondes.

DEAR ANNE – A few weeks ago, I met a pretty girl whom I liked immediately. We exchanged phone numbers, arranged a date, and spent a wonderful evening together, followed by a lovely afternoon a few days later. She told me she had recently been dropped by the man with whom she had lived for five years, had suffered a great deal and as a result might be 'stand-offish'. She said she certainly wouldn't be doing any of the chasing, so we arranged that I would call her. But now, I feel I am making all the running. I am used to my phone calls being returned and to being included in the life of the person I am dating. She has started telling her friends and family about me, but we do not see each other often, since she seems to be very busy. Should I forget about her and move on, or give her a break for a couple of weeks, as my intuition tells me?
J.F., Nottingham

Talk about a faint heart and a fair lady: it sounds as though you need a large dose of Irn Bru. You should expect to do the chasing, for goodness' sake: that's what men are for. Do you want her or don't you? If you don't care much either way, leave the poor girl to someone who does. She is feeling vulnerable and hurt, yet she has entrusted you with her problem and told you how to go about wooing her. What more do you want? Not returning your calls doesn't necessarily mean a girl isn't interested, but rather that she wants to know whether or not you are. After all, if she weren't, she'd hardly be telling her family about you, would she? Given her circumstances, it's highly likely that she needs to know how much you care: she has been treated badly and doesn't want it to happen again.

The best aphrodisiac, in my experience, is for a man to tell a woman that he finds her unbearably attractive, has been smitten to his very core, will never get over her and spends every moment of the day and night dreaming of her. (Yes, I know this can also be a massive turn-off. It all depends on the chap, and the halitosis. You just have to try it and see; that's what being a bloke is all about.) Though of course everything you say to her must also be completely and absolutely true. Otherwise you're just smarmy.

So, when she says she's busy for the week, leave her alone and try again seven days later – as your intuition tells you to. Clearly, if she'd said she was busy for six months, she would have been giving you a different message.

And if you can't get her on the telephone, turn up with the largest bunch of flowers you can find, a chilled bottle of Bolly and a couple of tickets for something. She will either tell you to get lost or melt on the spot: I'll bet a fiver on the latter.

Why in the name of goodness shouldn't you do all the running? Isn't that why God gave men longer legs?

DEAR ANNE – In all my 60-odd years, I have never, until I read your column, heard of Irn Bru. Is it the current slang for 'bottle', i.e. courage?
David Park, W. Sussex

I must apologize. I aim to keep in touch with other generations via my children and parents, but I'm obviously slipping. Last week, my father had to ask me to explain, not only Irn Bru, but also 'Bolly'. Both are drinks. Both give you oomph. One tastes rather better than the other.

DEAR ANNE – Thank you for telling me that Irn Bru is a drink that gives you oomph. But what is 'oomph'?
David Park, Staplefield, W. Sussex

A bit like pizzazz, it makes you funky, and helps to give you chutzpah. Hope that's clear now.

DEAR ANNE – 'Oomph'? 'Pizzazz'? 'Funky'? 'Chutzpah'? Is there no limit to my ignorance of the words which appear in your column? Perhaps it would be simpler if you just let me know the name of the dictionary to which I should refer.
David Park, W. Sussex

All in the second edition of Collins English Dictionary. Along with 'savvy'.

"I see your chutzpah is in excellent form today."

Extraordinarily, it would appear that not everyone prefers blondes. Particularly absent girlfriends.

**DEAR ANNE – My boyfriend sleeps with the dog while I am away. He claims he doesn't, but I know he does because I find her blonde hairs on the pillow.
B.D., London**

That's nothing. Sometimes, I sneak the dog into my side of the bed even when my husband is at home.

And anyway, what do you expect? It serves you right for leaving your boyfriend alone with a blonde.

DEAR ANNE – I have the perfect solution for dogs who insist on sleeping in the matrimonial bed.

**My answer to my wife sleeping with the dog was to build a kennel in the garden. Unfortunately, I'm the one sleeping in it.
Francis Lloyd, Ealing**

**DEAR ANNE – I enjoy reading your column, but I do wish you would stop writing about your disgusting habit of sleeping with your dog. Dogs have even more revolting and unhygienic habits than husbands, and I am amazed your husband has not booted both of you out of the bed, the room and the house.
M. Lyle, Lincoln**

I have passed your suggestion on to my husband, and he seems to be considering it.

There should probably be a Blonde Pride movement, to counter some of the discrimination and prejudice blondes suffer from …

**DEAR ANNE – One must marvel at the wisdom of nature when it comes to promoting the best of the species. In order to aid natural selection, it has apparently given English men a low sperm count and a taste for blondes. Continental men, who have no such predica-ment, prefer brunettes. Need I say more?
An Observer**

Funny. I've never noticed an aversion to blondes when I've been on the Continent. Or a low sperm count at home, come to think of it …

DEAR ANNE – On a first date, should you let a man pay if you only want to be friends?
A.T., London NW8

Whatever other pleasure you deny him, never deny a man the pleasure of paying.

We blondes have a saying: 'There is always such a thing as a free lunch.'